W9-AQS-682

# THOUGHTS ABOUT JIM MUNROE'S SHOW, THE MAZE:

Even though I am an Atheist, I still appreciate "The MAZE." Of course the magic illusions were amazingly thought provoking and skilled. It makes people of any belief system think more deeply about the world around them and how our own perception can become deception. Although the message about God and Jesus Christ did not get to me, it did reach a wide audience which was the main goal of the show, and it was certainly achieved.

**STUDENT**

Kansas State University—Manhattan, KS

Jim Munroe is a man whose mission is to present the gospel to a generation that is interested but cautious of religious tradition. He uses illusions to demonstrate that things are not always as they seem. He asks the "Why" and then inserts the truth of God's Word for all to consider. His program is a captivating presentation of "Why" and "How" that points to Jesus Christ as the answer.

**ROBERT MORRIS**

Founding Senior Pastor, Gateway Church—Southlake, TX

One of the most incredible ministries to teens today ... I fully support MAZE.

**RON LUCE**

Teen Mania Ministries—Tyler, TX

Having come to know the men of MAZE Ministries, I believe they have the greatest potential of any two people I know to carry on what I've been doing. I enthusiastically support them. They are on the cutting edge.

**ANDRE KOLE**

Illusionist, Magical Inventor of the Decade, David Copperfield Consultant

The MAZE will surprise, challenge and entertain you. I am a ... fan.

**MICHAEL WEBER**

Creative Producer for David Blaine,

Christopher Nolan's "Prestige," "The Illusionist"

Jim is a tremendously inspiring performer; he's walked the walk, and has lived to tell a wonderful story to those of us lucky enough to listen—very impressed!

**PAUL VIGIL**

Magician, Close-Up Magician of the Year, The Mirage—Las Vegas

As an Atheist, I was predisposed to not enjoy Jim's performances. Nothing pleases me more than to report the opposite. Jim's humble and pressure-free style offers his viewpoints in a way that allows his audience to think about things they may not have before. And most importantly, to question what is and what is not possible. Jim performs demonstrations that prove, in the right hands, miracles can happen.

**LUKE JERMAY**

Writer/Consultant, Criss Angel's "Mind Freak" Seasons 1, 2 & 3—

Las Vegas, NV

A staff member of The Navigators and a campus pastor have both been at the University of Maryland for 20+ years. Both of these men, individually, commented on the fact that the MAZE Outreach was the best outreach by far since they have been on campus.

**RYAN**

CRU—University of Maryland

MAZE is magically crazy. That dude needs to get a rabbit.

**MICHAEL JR**

Comedian—USA

I'm excited about this ministry. Having known [MAZE] for years, I have experienced their passion for the lost and the impact of their unique ministry. I believe it is a forerunner for the next generation of evangelism. They will blow you away!

**BILL MCCARTNEY**

Founder of PromiseKeepers

For further information please contact
Jim Munroe by visiting whatisthemaze.com
or write to the office of Mr. Munroe:

> 2150 E Continental Blvd.
> Southlake, TX 76092

**The Charlatan**
Copyright © 2012 by Jim Munroe
Photography (parts 1–3) by John Lynn
Published by Inprov, Ltd.

ISBN: 978-0-9833462-4-1
Printed in the United States of America.

# THE CHARLATAN

### THE SKEPTICAL,

### MYSTERIOUS,

### SUPERNATURAL TRUE

### STORY OF A CHRISTIAN

### MAGICIAN

## JIM MUNROE

## DEDICATION

---

**For Eli
Thank you for loving me.**

# ACKNOWLEDGEMENTS

Thank You, Lord Jesus, for Your continued grace. The story in the following pages is Yours, and I am privileged to be a small part. Thank You for letting me live this story. My greatest treasure is knowing You more fully. I cannot wait to know You fully just as I've been fully known.

This book would not be possible without the following wonderful people:

Thank you, Eli, for your love. I am the man I am today because of your unconditional love and support. Your selfless backing of MAZE has encouraged millions, and without you, none of this could be possible. For every moment I have been on the road, for every moment I was in the hospital, for every night I've been away ... thank you for your tremendous sacrifice. I love you more than you will ever know.

Thank you, Peyton and Gavin, for sharing your daddy with so many. You are a huge part of this ongoing story, and I think about you every minute of the day. I love you both so very, very much. I promise, one day, to teach you how I do some of these tricks.

Thank you, Jennell. I actually don't even know how to begin to thank you. Your gift of life continues to give to millions more. I'm so amazed at your courage and bravery. After my shows, I look into the eyes of so many young men and women who sign up to save a life. I cannot help but think about your choice to save a life and how it's changing the world for the better. You are the reason why my kids are not fatherless and my wife is not a widow. Thank you.

Thank you, Mom, for staying true to your passion and giving the beautiful gifts of the stage and the piano to your son. Everyone knows where I get it! I never got to the Wild Animal Park, but my dreams started on that rock. You are amazing, and I love you.

Thank you, Dad, for believing that I could be the best. It didn't happen on the mound, but because of that journey, I've never settled for second. You and Lee have a special place in my heart, and I love you both very much.

Hayley Jane ... I love you. You continue to blow me away with your awesomeness. All the brains went to you, and your talent knows no boundaries. Thank you for being the first responder and for all of your hard work to help me get to MD Anderson.

AJ and Susan Jacques ... I want you to know I firmly believe I have the greatest in-laws any human being could ever ask for. In the most difficult season of my life, you were beyond heroic. My family would not be what it is today without you. Thank you for circling the wagons and taking care of this Longhorn. I love you both very much.

Thank you, Tennyson McCarty, for believing that I could do what I do. I love you, and I miss you. When I see you again, we'll talk shop and I know you'll be proud of your MAZE.

Zak Mirzadeh, Daniel Cullen, and Sam Byers ... Thanks for putting up with a baseball coach of a boss. You guys are studs. This book doesn't happen without you.

Mr. Rob Domenech ... You're a brother. You've taught me so much. I am forever indebted.

Thank you, Brian and Marchelle, for always being a source of support to my family, especially through the tough times. I will never forget those weeks in 2007, but I'm thankful that we did it together. The Munroes love doing life with the Scaglias!

Thank you, Eric, Conrad, Chance, Somerset, and April McCarty. I am thankful to have known your amazing brother so well. I am also thankful for your continued support of MAZE.

Jed and Sara Walker ... Thank you for your belief in my family and me on so many levels. Jed, your talents and humility astound me.

Jimmy James, Brent Lamb, Lori Martin, and all the SMURFS ... THANK YOU! Thank you for believing in MAZE, even though I am crazy!

Thank you, Gresham Hill, Brad Fogarty, Kendall McDonald, Kyle Doan, and Hunter Day. MAZE isn't here without you.

My sincerest thanks to Jimmy and Patti Edwards, Doug and Marilee Schneider, Wayne and Cate Heck, Bob and Michele Fullmer, Casey and Cindy Journigan, and Dac and Donna Clark. You believed in this when nobody could. Thank you!

My greatest thanks to the MAZE partnership team! You know who you are! There is no MAZE Ministries without you. Your continued prayers and generous support have been amazing over the years. I love you guys very much!

A special thanks to Byron and Rachelle Copeland. I have never met people like you, and I thank you for being patient with me in the dark nights of the soul. You helped me go through so much, and I love you both.

Thank you, Todd Lane, Tom Lane, David Smith, Mark Jobe, Ed Funderburk, Craig Terndrup, Bob Hamp, and Robert Morris. The Lord dropped me off at your doorstep on Southlake Boulevard in October 2008, and I'm thankful for how you've ministered to me. I love being part of Team Gateway!

Andre and Kathy Kole, Larry Stephens, Jane Stump, Mark Gauthier, and everyone at CRU ... Thank you! You believed in MAZE when we were broken and crippled, and we are sharing His story with thousands because of that.

Thank you, Serban Maracine, Jordan Terrell, Jerret Sykes, and Joel Newton for walking with me.

Thank you to all of the CCA Family! You know who you are and you rock!

A BIG shout-out is in order for Morgan and Carrie Stephens, Bryan and Diane Schwartz, John and Chris Blue, Dave and April Jamerson (our original angel investors), Brad and Marina Butts, and Kevin and Sheri Irion. You believed in me. Thank you.

Thank you, Father Michael Pontarelli. I wouldn't have liked philosophy unless you were teaching it.

Thank you, Coach Tom Tereschuk and Coach Augie Garrido. You taught me how to win.

A special thanks to Dr. Debbie Thomas, Dr. Sirgio Girralt, and everyone at MD Anderson Cancer Center. You guys do the greatest job in the world, and I'm thankful that you cared as much as you did.

And last but not least, thank you, Rob Domenech (again), Michael Weber, Paul Vigil, and Jared Kopf. Bet you never thought you'd see your names in a book like this! Thank you for letting me be a fan of the greatest art form I have ever known. You guys blow me away!

# TABLE OF CONTENTS

# PROLOGUE

---

*"He who can no longer pause to wonder and stand rapt in awe, is as good as dead; his eyes are closed."*

Albert Einstein

I know something you don't know—something you would never tell your friends, something you don't consciously think about, something you're not willing to tweet, text, or post on your Facebook page.

But I already know your secret, and I've built my life's work on it.

I know because I've seen it in hundreds of dark theaters filled with excited anticipation before the video rolls and the lights come up.

I know because I've witnessed it firsthand in the courtyards of the most prestigious academic centers in the world where skepticism, secularism, and the scientific process rule.

And I know because I've even experienced it in the executive boardrooms of corporate America where power, productivity, and the bottom line have the final say.

Here's your secret: You want me to trick you. You want, more than anything else, to be amazed.

I know, I know. It's true. But don't worry—I'm not going to tell anyone. I'm not going to embarrass you. Your name isn't going to be posted on a blog alongside thousands of other "marks."

You can try and deny it if you want, but you have a secret longing to be awed, to be captivated, to be filled with wonder. For just a moment, you want life to transcend what you can perceive with your senses and logically figure out with your mind. This doesn't make you a sucker, a simpleton, or a mouth breather. It doesn't mean you're not intelligent, respectable, or professional.

It just means you're human.

We have a deal, you and I. I realize we never sat down and signed a contract, but this agreement is very real. It's a social contract. For a few moments, I remind you that you're not in control. Of course, deep down, you already know this is true—I just make it okay for you to remember.

And here's the truth—I know you feel this way because deep down, I feel it, too. It's the whole reason I got into magic in the first place.

I love being amazed.

I think it's a quintessential part of our human experience. It doesn't matter where you're from, how educated you are, how much money you have, or how old you are—you want to be connected to the mysterious and the supernatural.

With all of our progress, education, scientific accomplishments, and technological advances, it's easy to lose sight of the fact that our universe is absolutely teeming with mystery. There's so much we don't know. Our most learned and intelligent thinkers can't explain so many of the things we do understand.

The most powerful and successful among us, those with resources beyond what most of us can imagine, live with the illusion of control. Having a fleet of private planes and owning your own island in the South Pacific creates the mirage of unlimited power, but none of those things can stave off death, cancer, or even the deepest longings of the human heart.

Those aren't words to me—I've experienced this truth firsthand.

That's why you need me. You want someone to remind you of the awe-inspiring unknown that surrounds all of us, all the time. It's right there in front of you, but you need someone to show you where to look.

Let me show you what I'm talking about.

Go back to the first page. Stare directly into the center of the page. Focus your eyes and look behind the letters. Once your eyes have adjusted, I want you to find the third letter of the fourth word on every line of the first page.

I'll say it again: The third letter of the fourth word on every line.

Keep writing down these letters until you have at least ten letters. In these letters, you'll find a word scramble that will reveal your name.

See for yourself. I'm not going anywhere. Seriously. Take a minute and try it. I'll be here when you're done.

Did you find it? I know what you're thinking: That's impossible. There are thousands of names out there, and this book has already been printed. How could I possibly know what your name is?

But if you looked, you proved my point whether or not you find your name. You want to be amazed.

I know this because I have a secret, too. And just like you, I don't tell my friends, and I refuse to tweet, text, or post my secret on my Facebook page.

Until now.

The truth is—I'm a charlatan—someone who pretends to have

more knowledge or skills in his profession than he actually possesses. It's all an act. I don't have any psychic abilities or magical powers, but I'm not using hidden cameras, recording devices, or crowd plants. It takes genuine skill to weave mystery, the unknown, and a sense of wonder to such a compelling degree that it overpowers your skepticism—not just anyone can do it.

"Charlatan" is an old 16th Century French word derived from the Italian word for "prattle" or "chatter" like a duck … or a quack. From its origin, the word has carried a negative connotation, but the reality is, you can find charlatans in every profession.

The best charlatans are all magicians—filmmakers, comic book writers, professional wrestlers, improvisational comedians, etc.— and they're willing to embrace the social contract. You give us your attention, and we give you permission to indulge your imagination. You give us your suspended disbelief, and we tell you a magical tale, we craft an experience that allows you to embrace that child-like sense of wonder that makes you feel alive.

The ones you have to watch out for—Ponzi schemes, corrupt politicians, personal injury lawyers, snake oil salesmen, etc.—won't ever break the fourth wall. They refuse to let you behind the curtain. They'll look you right in the eye and tell you there is no curtain. You're never going to get control of the relationship.

A charlatan looks for a "mark"—a spectator who's emotionally excitable, expressive, and ready and willing to be taken for a ride. The reason is simple—not only will this spectator go where you take him, but his passion and commitment to the process will influence others to buy in, too. Once you understand a little psychology and learn how people are wired, it's fairly easy to spot a mark.

Don't think that I'm patronizing or belittling this person. We're all grateful to have "marks" in our lives—they make the most encouraging friends, motivated volunteers, caring spouses, and attentive parents.

I should know—I've been looking for great spectators all my life.

I love the adrenaline that comes from taking the audience on a journey—and throughout the course of my life, I've used all kinds of vehicles: a grand piano, the pages of a play, a baseball, a deck of cards, a podium and microphone, and even a stuffed bear named Cocoa.

At the most basic level, the real power of magic is its ability to show us our world is bigger and more mysterious than we imagined. It takes away some of our most basic defenses—our intellectual superiority, our natural desire for knowledge, and the illusion of our control. I don't like to give those things up. Most magicians don't. If there's anything we can spot, it's another charlatan. We know his next move before he makes it because it would be our next move, too.

We know so much about you, because in so many ways, we are you, or at least, we used to be you. I've given my life to identifying and perfecting ways to connect with your deepest psychological longings in such an awe-inspiring way that you're convinced it's magic even when everything inside is saying, "There's no way!"

Countless hours have been spent to understand what makes you tick so I can discover the secrets to shock and amaze you. But the price I pay to give you this thrill is great. To fill you with a sense of awe, I end up losing my own. It's a cruel irony.

David Copperfield once said, "To become a magician means to give up wonder."

Penn Jillette said, "You get into magic because you love being tricked. The longer you do it, the harder it is to get fooled. You miss that. It's like chasing that first high."

Penn and his partner Teller were so serious about reclaiming this sense of wonder that they created a contest they filmed as a TV series titled, *Fool Us*. The prize was a contract as the opening act for the Penn & Teller show in Las Vegas.

All magicians start out with the joy and wonder of a spectator. It's why we got into magic in the first place. But once you become the performer, once you get used to telling the story, it's very difficult to go back. The distance from center stage to the front row is miles longer from our side of the theater. It's completely unnatural for anyone in any profession to voluntarily surrender control once he's used to having it.

Most magicians believe that life just is—there's nothing magical or supernatural or mysterious. It's just data we don't have access to, a perspective that's been hidden from us through clever planning with masterful skill. Once someone shows us what was right in front of us all along, the supernatural becomes our ordinary, easily explained reality. We trade our "Oooohs" and "Aaaahs" for an "Oh."

There's no great and powerful wizard behind the curtain—just a cynical little man with a megaphone, colored smoke, and a few mechanical levers.

I never thought that's where my road would lead, until one day from behind the curtain, I realized that I'd lost the ability to be amazed.

Behind every mystery, I saw fingerprints and clues leading to a rational, completely natural explanation.

And in that place, I discovered life without wonder wasn't worth living.

I believe this explains why so many in the magic community are fascinated with death and angered by the conventional characterizations of God. When I first started in magic, I never imagined I would feel that way, but I lived in that place for more than two years. It became my home, my world.

The only thing more shocking was what happened next. It was terrifying, beyond my greatest fears, unimaginably more difficult than what I ever thought I could endure.

To get back the wonder, I had to take the long walk from the stage to the seat, from being the performer to being the spectator, from being the one in control allowing the audience to see only what I wanted them to see, to being the one who had no control over anything.

In other words, in order to be amazed, I had to lose everything. I had to die. Not as an illusion, not an elaborate trick, no sleight of hand.

The only way back to life was through death.

My prayer is as you read the incredible, awe-inspiring mysteries that have been my life, you'll discover the amazing wonder in your own.

# PART ONE

The magician shows you something ordinary.

# CHAPTER 1

---

# THE NEXT GREAT ... SOMEBODY!

*"The suspense is terrible ... I hope it will last."*

Gene Wilder as Willy Wonka,

*Willy Wonka & the Chocolate Factory*

I was born for the stage—it's in my blood.

I came into this world in pursuit of a microphone and an audience. I always imagined if I could get one, the other would follow.

I turned anything into a microphone; some things like a wooden spoon, a plastic knife, or a broken radio antenna were easy. But it didn't really matter. You could give me a rock, a toy car, or a shoe. As far as I was concerned, you were asking me to perform.

Once I had my microphone, I believed the world was anxiously waiting for me. I actually have an old VHS tape of one of my earliest, backyard acoustic sets. You might see a two-year-old kid standing on a large rock in his backyard, but in my mind, the venue was every bit as prestigious as Radio City Music Hall or the Hollywood Bowl.

When most kids go to Sea World or the San Diego Wild Animal Park, they want to be one of the trainers so they can touch the beautiful, breath-taking animals. Not me. I longed for a microphone and an audience.

If you're still not getting how serious I was about this, maybe this will help. Like most kids, I loved movies. But while my friends' favorites were huge blockbusters like *Star Wars*, *Ghostbusters*, or *Indiana Jones*, I loved Neil Diamond's *The Jazz Singer* more than all the rest.

If you've never had the privilege of watching this cinematic classic, let me assure you, it's cheesy 1980s filmmaking at its finest. It follows the story of a small club singer who struggles to make it to the big time. The film is filled with live concert performances, and if you look past the sequin jackets, frilly scarves, and almost inhuman amounts of chest hair, you see that the power of a performer captivating his audience is really compelling. When Neil belts out the finale, *"... They're coming to A-MER-I-CAAA ...,"* you'll realize why the dude is still touring and selling out arenas 30 years later.

My parents recognized and nurtured my love for the stage early on, taking me to see all kinds of performers. Every year, they bought family season passes to a local theatre—The La Mirada Theatre for the Performing Arts. I remember watching community productions of Broadway plays, fairy tales like *Little Red Riding Hood* and *Hansel and Gretel*, and a concert from the one and only Don McLean. He was no Neil Diamond, but he did drive the Chevy to the levy.

But one of those performances didn't just leave a lasting memory ... it changed my life. It wasn't the first time I'd been to the theatre, but something was different this time. On a beautiful Sunday afternoon, that theatre wasn't a playhouse or a concert hall.

That day, the cushy, crimson, velvet theatre seats transported me to a supernatural, mysterious world: *my first magic show*!

♣ ♦ ♥ ♠

The nervous energy and anticipation were so strong, I felt like I had to pee—and I'd already made a trip to the little boys' room. As the lights dimmed and the massive red curtain opened, a single spotlight illuminated a large, hollow Plexiglas box in the middle of the stage.

A young woman effortlessly moved the box forward then spun it around so we could see no one was behind it and nothing was attached to it. She also waved her hand around in the box to demonstrate nothing was inside. Mom told me later this young woman was beautiful, but I hardly noticed her. I couldn't take my eyes off the giant, transparent container.

Without warning, a thick cloud of smoke erupted inside the box, completely filling the canister. My five-year-old mind was blown. I thought the smoke was the trick until a human hand darted through the smoke and slammed against the clear wall. Now you may have guessed this hand belonged to a man who appeared in the box, but I did not see it coming.

It was almost too much for me to handle.

The show had only begun, and my tiny brain couldn't process the information fast enough. My mouth was frozen open in a perpetual state of awe. As the man stepped out of the Plexiglas container, he spread his arms and bowed to greet the audience as it erupted in a roar of applause and cheers.

His appearance was so spectacularly dramatic, when he introduced himself, all I heard was *"The Great ... Somebody."*

I ran into the same magician, performing on the streets at Universal Studios in my teenage years, but all these years later, I still don't remember his name. I guess that first impression was too overwhelming.

He wore a midnight black tuxedo with tails—the standard issue outfit of every great old-school magician. His voice boomed and reverberated in all its baritone glory.

*"Are you ready for a fantastic afternoon? Then let's begin!"*

What?!? I couldn't believe it. After seeing him emerge from a closed, clear container through billowing thick smoke, I would have gone home happy. That was only the beginning? In the ninety minutes that followed, my world shifted on its axis. The boundaries of reality and impossibility were redefined before my very eyes.

- *Doves materialized and flew from empty hands.*
- *The beautiful assistant was sawed in half and instantaneously put back together with the wave of his hand.*
- *A freshly cracked egg transformed into a parakeet.*
- *A woman levitated six feet above his head then vanished into thin air.*

And finally, *The Great ... Somebody* was chained and shackled in a large, black coffin only to vanish and reappear in the back of the theatre behind us.

More than 25 years later, those initial moments remain in my imagination. It took only a few moments of witnessing the secrets of the universe being manipulated in front of us to reach past my orange and blue striped polo and captivate the deepest recesses of my heart.

My life purpose was clear: I wanted to be a magician. No. It was much stronger than that. I HAD to be a magician. I had no say in the matter.

I would become the next, the better, the more sensational *Great ... Somebody!*

♣ ♦ ♥ ♠

The first step in my transformation came through an unlikely source. Grandma Dot had heard about my life-changing experience, and she wanted to help me achieve my greatest purpose in life.

For my sixth birthday, she gave me the building block every great illusionist and master of the dark arts begins with: The Fisher-Price Magic Set. It had everything a burgeoning child magician would need to begin to hone his skills—three red sponge balls, a long multi-colored trick handkerchief, a magic-wand with a pop-out fake flower, and a plastic dove.

I had a few initial successes. My four-year-old sister was flabber-gasted ... when she actually paid attention. Mom could barely handle the level of illusion and sorcery her six-year-old prodigy served up, even though she read the instruction manual for me.

Quickly, the limitations of my kit appeared. The more I tried to create shows, the lamer they seemed. I tried to fight off discouragement, but I was too frustrated. I wasn't some hack who did this as a hobby. I was destined to be a great magician.

Grandma Dot's Fisher-Price kit didn't help me appear in a closed, Plexiglas container through a thick cloud of smoke. I couldn't make the plastic dove disappear, much less make real doves fly out of my empty hand. Forget sawing a beautiful assistant in half and putting her back together, I couldn't even saw my little sister in half.

This wasn't what I'd given my life, my future, and my talents for. Where was the danger? Where was the sense of mystery? Where was the thrill of terrible anticipation?

Neil Diamond wasn't the only sequined-clad performer who inspired me. I was also captivated by Willy Wonka. In his wonderful world, you had the sense something dangerous and mysterious was happening right in front of you. The trick was realizing where to look.

This was the sense of anticipation I was trying so hard to create, and yet, my Fisher-Price kit couldn't deliver. But I wanted it so badly, I was determined to keep trying.

♣ ♦ ♥ ♠

One of my favorite filmmakers, J.J. Abrams, told a story about a magic box at the TED Conference in 2007. When he was a teenager, his grandfather took him to Lou Tannen's magic shop located in a crappy little building in Midtown Manhattan. But when the elevator doors opened, visitors were immediately in the magic shop—a world of mystery, suspense, and the impossible. It was a magical place.

The store had all kinds of magic tricks—complex ones for experienced performers and simple, classic illusions for beginners. One thing they sold was "Tannen's Mystery Magic Box," featuring $50 worth of magic tricks for just $15. Abrams bought it but never opened it. He told the audience he's not a pack rat, but he's always kept that box with him, wherever he's gone, because of what it represents.

> " ... It represents infinite possibility. It represents hope. It represents potential. And what I love about this box, and what I realize I sort of do in whatever it is that I do, is I find myself drawn to infinite possibility, that sense of potential. And I realize that mystery is the catalyst for imagination. Now it's not the most ground-breaking idea, but when I started to think that maybe there are times where mystery is more important than knowledge ... "

Abram's words have resonated with me—and not because I'm a huge fan of his work. He articulated something I'd always known but struggled to communicate.

The thrill of magic isn't in the illusions themselves. Once you have the knowledge to create an illusion and the skill to execute it perfectly, something is lost. There's something about the mystery, the anticipation, and the experience. There's a deeper human longing to be amazed or awed that you're trying to connect with.

My Fisher-Price kit, as limited as it was and even though I'd opened it, had served its purpose. Like "Tannen's Mystery Magic Box," it showed me a glimmer of possibility, the faintest crack of potential.

♣ ♦ ♥ ♠

As I got older, I expressed myself in other performance arenas. I attended a Catholic private school, which held an annual lip-sync rally with quite the local reputation. Collaborating with a couple of other first-graders, we brought down the house with our rendition of Ray Parker, Jr.'s classic, *Ghostbusters*.

We *"weren't 'fraid of no ghosts"*—and I wasn't afraid of the crowd's loving approval. I was a performer at heart. The two-year old singing from his backyard rock stage hadn't lost his love of center stage.

The hunger was growing.

Nothing provided the thrill and adrenaline that magic did. I bought magic how-to VHS tapes, checked out library books on card tricks, and spent most of my childhood requesting birthday and Christmas presents that promised to make me a master of the magical arts. I devoured everything I could get my hands on and practiced until I could complete the tricks seamlessly.

I loved giving people the same feeling the nameless magician had given me. Providing people with wonder and awe is a gift. It can turn even the hardest skeptic into a child, if only for a moment.

When I was 10, I realized all my hard work and practice may have finally developed into a craft. Up to that point, my parents thought my magic was a nice little hobby for their son. It was cute.

But when I made a spoon bend with my mind, then break, then disappear from open hands not hidden by sleeves, they went completely silent. The room was still for a long, awkward pause. They both sat there with their mouths opened ... then shouted with awestruck amazement.

And that was it. I'd tasted what it felt like to offer wonder, awe, and mystery to others. I couldn't get enough. I was ready to give my life to become the next *Great ... Somebody*.

I'd experienced the power of performing, but I had no idea it came at such a high price.

# CHAPTER 2

---

# EVERYTHING AND NOTHING

*"There is no such thing as 'fun for the whole family.'"*

Jerry Seinfeld

There's no county in the United States that people love more than Orange County.

It's where everybody wants to be. It's ground zero for the American dream—stunning beaches, perfect weather, the latest food, fashions, music and culture, and home to all the beautiful people. You can go surfing and skiing on the same day.

And I grew up there before it was famous.

Long before Bravo unleashed seven horrific seasons of the *Real Housewives of Orange County* upon the American public. Before Lauren, Spencer, and Heidi televised their planned, scripted, and choreographed high school "reality" on MTV's *Laguna Beach* and *The Hills*. Before Jack Black's burst onto the comedy scene, running around in his underwear as Collin Hank's hilariously delusional brother in the underrated movie, *Orange County*. And, of course, even before FOX's ridiculous teen drama, *The O.C.* No one living in Orange County calls it *"The O.C."* The show's creator was from Providence, Rhode Island.

Orange County was my home, and as a kid, it felt like living in a dream world. It's surreal. You don't go to Disneyland for vacation ... you go there on Friday after school. You play outside year round—it's like a 75-degree summer vacation that never ends.

Dad built a full-size batting cage for me in our backyard to go with the pitcher's mound we created using the natural slope on our lot. With over 20 orange trees on our property, we could actually have fresh-squeezed orange juice without going to the store.

We had a pool, a Jacuzzi, a trampoline—everything a kid could want. It's almost a little too good to be true. As if all these blessings weren't enough, we lived a short drive away from some truly incredible beaches. As a kid, I spent every Tuesday and Thursday at Corona del Mar—an absolutely breath-taking spot people come from all over the world to see.

I thought it was normal.

♣ ♦ ♥ ♠

As far back as I can remember, I had a season pass to Disneyland, one of the most significant backdrops of my youth. That's where we went for "family time." It's still Mom's favorite place to go when we're all together.

On several occasions, I remember my parents surprising us at school and pulling us from classes to hang out with Mickey and his friends. Even as I got older, Disneyland was still cool—my friends and I would see how many people we could get in on one pass.

When I think back to those days, I understand why everybody wants to live there, why there's such a demand to experience the lifestyle even from afar.

My parents were from Southern California. Dad's extended family spread throughout Texas and Washington. His parents met while my grandfather was serving in WWII. Like so many other young soldiers, when he came back to the states, he wanted a piece of paradise, so he settled in California.

My grandmother (on my dad's side) was from East Texas, and she grew up without a lot of running water. The rapidly expanding suburbs of the San Fernando Valley in the 1950s provided a quality of life beyond her dreams.

Across my family tree, Mom grew up in La Mirada, an inland city in Orange County with a well-known Christian college. La Mirada occasionally shows up on one of those best places to live lists because people care about their community.

La Mirada means "the view," and it was home to the performing arts center where I encountered *The Great ... Somebody!* which changed the trajectory of my life. Mom's dad died when she was only five years old, and my grandmother remarried not long after to the man I knew as "Grandpa" my whole life.

I never met Mom's dad, but as I got older, everyone in the family told me how much I looked like him. As a kid, when a great-aunt or grandmother tells you this, you smile, but you don't really know what to say. It's hard to relate to.

But as the years went by, our similar appearance would no longer be the greatest bond between us. My grandfather died of cancer at the age of 35.

My parents met when they were both students at Southern California College of Optometry in nearby Fullerton. It doesn't sound all that romantic, but they must have spent enough time studying/staring into each other's eyes to fall in love.

Their partnership extended beyond the home to the office. They shared their own optometry practice, which meant they could alternate their schedules so one of them was always home for us. Even though they were very hard working, professional people with a lot of responsibility, they created a really stable home environment.

♣ ♦ ♥ ♠

We did all the things that every kid hopes his family will do, even if he doesn't admit it around his friends. We ate dinner together every evening, spent game night together playing UNO, and laughed together at the Cosby Show as a family. The Huxtables were just like us—their parents were both professionals, and they always looked like they were laughing and having fun together. But while the Huxtables lived in Brooklyn, we got to live in Orange County.

We had it all—we were the perfect family.

Because of my parents' flexible work schedules, Dad coached every one of my sports teams until I was in high school. He loved sports—his brother and his dad were coaches, too. He also coached all of my sister's softball and basketball teams. He was always there, coaching us through every team practice, then he spent many more hours working with us one-on-one after everybody else went home, fine-tuning our swing or the fundamentals of shooting a basketball.

He was hard on us and instilled a strong work ethic, but he wasn't a taskmaster. He wasn't living vicariously through our athletic accomplishments to make up for his own shortcomings. It was simply one of the ways he loved to spend time with us.

All those hours of practice and games started to take their toll on Mom. Over time, my parents grew further and further apart. I didn't see it as it was happening. From a distance, it looked like they were sharing everything, but what started as a genuine partnership drifted to become more of a division of individual responsibilities.

As the Orange County playbook for a perfect family dictates, the number of hours devoted to practices and games piled up, and kids' sports became the axis around which our lives revolved. My mom was a competitor, but she wasn't an athlete, and I think the sports wore her down.

♣ ♦ ♥ ♠

My mom is an artist, a student of life, and she always has a new hobby or interest. She's been a champion quilter, been fascinated with exotic birds, loves the arts, and took us to Broadway plays. I'll never forget the time she surprised my sister and me by pulling us out of school to take the long drive to Ahmanson Theatre in downtown Los Angeles to see the original cast in *Phantom of the Opera.*

She couldn't help me throw a curveball or teach me how to dribble with my left hand, but she was determined to invest in me.

Inspiring a love for the arts, developing my skills, and providing creative outlets were responsibilities she took very seriously. Every year, she directed the Lip-Sync Rally at our school where I first learned the rush of adrenaline that comes from captivating an audience. She forced me to take piano lessons, and I fought her with the same arsenal of whining, complaining, and pouty protests that all athletic boys throw back at piano-loving moms. But she didn't give in—she saw talent in me I couldn't appreciate then.

My piano teacher terrified me. Nadine Munt was old—so old, in fact, that she'd been my mom's teacher when she was a kid. She wouldn't let me play Chopsticks with my index fingers like most kids. I had to work on Gershwin, Joplin, Chopin, Beethoven, Mozart, Bach, and Handel. She may have been old enough to be their high school classmates, but Mrs. Munt scared me into practicing the old masters until they became friends of mine, too.

Between Mrs. Munt's and my mom's efforts, I was at that piano at 6:20 every morning for an hour of practice. My fingers were moving, but my mind was still asleep. Initially, I hated it, but over time, they wore me down. I developed a genuine love for the music and the joy that came from playing a beautifully constructed piece on the piano.

While my mom encouraged my artistic abilities, Dad continued to help mold my baseball skills. He had the highest aspirations for my future, and we'd talk about me playing in the big leagues one day as a matter of when, not if.

Looking back now, the tension was obvious, but in the moment, I didn't see any of the signs. There were no knock-down/drag-out fights between my parents. No threats or ultimatums. But under the surface, our American dream was drifting beyond the point of repair. We weren't like the Huxtables after all.

After 17 years of marriage, my parents decided the breach was too great. The practice, the home, the dream life, and even my sister and I weren't enough to keep them together. They were getting a divorce.

♣ ♦ ♥ ♠

I was completely blind-sided. It felt like my legs were cut out beneath me. The stability that had been such a unique, wonderful blessing came crumbling down, and as a fifteen year-old kid, I didn't handle it well.

Fifteen is a tough age anyway. On any given day, you're a powder keg of hormones, emotions, curiosity, and stupidity capable of doing serious damage to both your well-being and your future. At that stage in life, everything is appearance. You don't want to look different than your friends, and yet now, everything was going to be different.

One day at school, emotions overwhelmed me, and I lost it in the bathroom. I was so distraught, an administrator called my dad to come get me. My dad tried to encourage me and explained how very sorry he was, but our family had to change.

I couldn't accept it. This wasn't supposed to happen. Our loving home environment had been the single greatest source of stability and support in my world, and now it was gone.

What about all our family time at Disneyland? It never turned out this way in the movies or at the park. Prince Charming never grew distant from Snow White because he liked sports and she didn't. Sleeping Beauty and the Prince weren't trying to make it work for the sake of the kids. They loved each other.

I couldn't make sense of it. My fifteen-year-old capacity to trust quickly began to erode. I started second-guessing everything as my heart and mind became increasingly skeptical. My burgeoning love for magic was teaching me the power of illusion and deception. I was also developing a love for philosophy and psychology. Both offered complex explanations for why things appeared to be one way but, in reality, were fundamentally different.

All these factors came together with powerful force.

Angry, frustrated, and hurt, I began to lash out at the trust and confidence of others in a vain attempt to numb my own pain. It was petty and vindictive, but it made me feel better.

The rest of the country may have wanted my Orange County life, but I didn't.

And once you have everything, and then realize it's nothing, somewhere deep down, you start to lose hope there's anything truly worth having.

# CHAPTER 3

---

# FAST TIMES AT SERVITE HIGH

*"I keep looking at the sky, 'cause it's gettin' me high/*
*forget the hearse 'cause I'll never die/ I got nine lives/*
*Cat's eyes/ Usin' every one of them and runnin' wild"*
AC/DC, "Back in Black"

Dealing with divorce sucks—especially when you've spent your whole life in the perfect family.

No more dinner together every night. No more laughing and playing UNO. No more spontaneous getaways to Disneyland. Now you have to pick sides. Yeah, yeah—you love both of them, but deep down you feel the pressure to pick Team Mom or Team Dad.

And now you get to watch them awkwardly figure out their new "normal"—*Do we celebrate birthdays together? Where do we go for Christmas? What do I call that person I'm dating, and how/when do I introduce him/her to the kids?*

Good times.

You know what makes this even more fun? Working through this as a freshman in high school. You remember your freshman year, right?

First year in high school … figuring out where you're supposed to go first period, working hard to fit in at the new school with new classmates, hoping not to embarrass yourself and get a terrible nickname that sticks with you for four years … or the rest of your life.

All the while hormones course through your body, causing you to think and say things that make you sound like a crazy person. Most days it's like your sole purpose in life is to be the victim or the punch line for the latest upperclassmen prank.

But being really good at baseball and having limited parental supervision tends to make life more manageable.

♣ ♦ ♥ ♠

All my parents really wanted from me was to perform—get good grades in the classroom and excel on the baseball field. That wasn't a problem. By the middle of my freshman year, I started to get recruitment and scholarship letters from some of the country's most prestigious universities.

With Mom and Dad feeling great about my future, I had every opportunity to take full advantage of my newfound freedom. Between my high school, Area Code, and Scout Teams, I played baseball year round.

When young men spend that much time together away from parental supervision, they tend to focus on three things: sex, alcohol, and drugs. It's what you talk about in the locker room while you're getting ready for practice. It's what you joke about while you're stretching, taking batting practice, or messing with each other in the dugout. You joke about it on road trips. You dare each other to go further when you're out at night with the guys. And you exaggerate the details of your adventures and escapades to each other the next day.

Most people don't realize it, but among the players, these three subjects are as much a part of baseball's culture as the seventh inning stretch and "Take Me Out to the Ballgame." Fortunately, before things got too out of hand, I had a bad experience that scared me away from some of the harder drugs.

In the summer before my junior year, KROQ, one of the more popular radio stations in Southern California, held an annual concert/party sarcastically called "The Weenie Roast and Sing-a-Long" in Irvine. It sounds like good, old-fashioned SoCal fun hosted by the Beach Boys, but it was much darker than that. Sublime, Rage Against the Machine, and the Ramones headlined the event that summer.

To this day, I'm not even sure what I smoked. I think it was PCP. Whatever it was, it freaked me out. When I walked, I couldn't feel my legs, and I got the strange sensation I was floating and drifting away from my body. It was terrifying. I grew increasingly more paranoid that I would lose complete control and float away into space.

It was one of those moments when you tell yourself, *"If I can just calm down and feel normal, I'll NEVER do that again."* After that experience, I was done experimenting—I'd stick with the proven essentials—weed, beer, and liquor.

♣ ♦ ♥ ♠

Most of my good friends in high school were my teammates, and to understand them, you had to understand my school. Servite High School is an all-boys, Roman Catholic, college prep school in Anaheim. It's not your typical high school. Ninety-nine percent of graduates continue on to college. College is a given, and athletes believe a great career at a Division 1 school and even the big leagues of professional sports are within reach.

It wasn't a dream—it's what seniors and alumni had done for decades.

All my friends were dealing with the same issues—struggling with the impact of divorce, adjusting to the intense academic and athletic demands of our new school, and learning to handle rising levels of testosterone. If you didn't know us, you'd think we were a bunch of cocky punks, but to our families and our teachers, we were gifted young leaders with great potential.

The truth is, we were both.

We were intelligent, talented, and aware of the high expectations our families had for us—and we had for ourselves. Partying and drinking took our minds off these issues ... so we drank a lot.

Like every weekend.

After our Friday night game, we'd drink hard enough to ensure a massive hangover, sleep wherever we were, and then get up and do it again. I'm amazed I survived those years. When you're young, you think you're indestructible, but life has a way of pointing out just how fragile it is—a lesson I would learn all too well only a few short years later.

Servite was a Catholic school, and none of the guys in my group of friends had any moral or religious objections to how we were living. In our minds, getting drunk, smoking weed, and having sex didn't keep us from being *"good Catholics,"* as long as we went to Mass and to confession every so often. There were many genuine, devout Catholics at the school, but we were never counted among the faithful.

Our school was only a few exits down the freeway from Disney-land, but the kid who grew up going to see Mickey and riding the teacups with his family was a long way from the young man who made the Varsity baseball team as a freshman.

Spending all my time around guys, I had very little understanding of how to behave like a gentleman. It was difficult to learn how to treat a lady at an all-guys school. I did learn how to mess with my teachers and pull pranks. Sometimes this was the same thing.

My Spanish teacher happened to be an Asian-American (*I know it sounds crazy, but it's not uncommon in Southern California*). We thought it would be hilarious if we swapped all of our "La"s for "Ra"s as a clever homage to her heritage. She didn't think it was so funny.

Some of our classes were taught by priests, and we made fun of them, too. High school boys aren't known for their discretion or self-control. A smart, seasoned priest knew the best way to fight back was to come right at us. I'll never forget—one priest told us he hoped heaven was like one big orgasm since he'd waited his whole life not to have one. We couldn't think of a comeback. (And it should be noted, he no longer works at the school.)

♣ ♦ ♥ ♠

I wasn't a dumb jock—none of my friends were. We really enjoyed school. From my earliest days at Servite, I remember being challenged to think critically—an approach I already valued, at least, in part, because of my love for magic and illusion. The same curiosity and wonder that drew me to the stage kept me interested in the classroom.

My favorite subjects were philosophy and ethics, and I was fascinated by the social and cultural dynamics of morality. I was really influenced by the concept of moral relativism—the idea that a belief, behavior, or value may be good and true for one person but not for someone else. This notion felt mysterious and puzzling, which made it only more intriguing.

My passion for magic continued to grow. I carried a deck of cards with me everywhere constantly shuffling them in my hands. I practiced to disguise the sound with other ambient noise to avoid the attention of my teachers.

Even midway through that first season, college coaches were in the stands any time I was on the mound, but around school, my reputation as a magician was developing as quickly as my prominence as a pitcher. I elicited *"Oohs"* and *"Aaahhs"* from teachers and students alike with my ever-growing arsenal of illusions.

In some ways, I enjoyed that attention more because I didn't have to share it with any of my teammates.

My AP English teacher, Mr. Eccelston, was also an aspiring illusionist. He had bright white hair, a white beard, and reading glasses perched half-way down his nose. He would stare at me through his glasses, leaning in so I could see his pack of unfiltered PALL MALL cigarettes (you could still smoke in the state of California back then) popping out of his shirt pocket, and ask me rhetorically, *"Do you believe in magic?"*

One day, he brought a pail of water to class, and after he asked me the question, he passed his hand over the water. As he did, the water jumped to life in the bucket, splashing around. Of course, now I know how he did it, but back then, it was simply incredible, and it strengthened my love for magic.

I chased that feeling wherever I could find it. Sometimes the pursuit led me to the one good side to being at an all-boys school—the two all-girls Catholic sister schools in our area. But I also found magic on the baseball diamond.

It's a good thing that our school had an established history of athletic dominance, including league and state championships, because our mascot was (and still is) "The Friars." Remember "Friar Tuck" from *Robin Hood*—the fat guy in robes with a bowl cut? Not exactly the most intimidating character.

During my time at Servite, our mascot received a face-lift. His robe went over his head, the jolly fat guy became two red slit eyes, and he carried a "scythe," a creepy harvesting tool loved by death metal bands.

I thought it was a little strange that we were still called "The Friars" when our mascot went from being a fat priest to the Grim Reaper, but we didn't care. The new logo had more street cred—both with high school boys and biker gangs.

Our black uniforms were accented with just a bit of white, and we'd always blare AC/DC's "Back in Black" while warming up for home games. AC/DC was the same '80s metal band that sang "Highway to Hell," "Hell's Bells," and "You Shook Me All Night Long"—not exactly "Ave Maria." I'm not sure why the priests allowed AC/DC to represent their fine Catholic institution of higher learning, but I guess, as long as we won, they didn't care.

"Back in Black" has one of the best guitar riffs ever, and anyone who's ever competed athletically knows the incredible adrenaline surge you get right before a game starts. The song perfectly captured the ecstatic sense of being young, fearless, and powerful.

I enjoyed school and I loved magic, but baseball was my life. It framed my identity and provided my self-worth—and if the hundreds of college letters I was receiving were any indication, I was worth a lot.

Years of hard work, talented genes, quality coaching, and my father's guidance had positioned me for the big leagues.

I had so many college offers that I began to throw some away. *"What's that Notre Dame? You want me to come to South Bend, Indiana, to play baseball for you? In the freezing cold? I don't think so."*

After sifting through all the collegiate options, I started to entertain ideas about skipping college and turning professional right out of high school.

♣ ♦ ♥ ♠

Although I was living with my dad, my mom still had a big influence in my life, and she did not like this idea at all. It wasn't because baseball was the biggest bond I shared with my father and, at times, had made her feel distanced from both of us. She greatly values education and thought I was too gifted academically to ignore that part of my ongoing development.

But there was another influential voice in the process as well.

My on-again, off-again girlfriend of four years was a very important influence in my life. I had dreams of going to college together with her. She came into my life at a time when I really needed someone as I continued to struggle with my changing family dynamics.

During all the transition, my family attended a Lutheran church.

My parents were trying to provide some spiritual support for us, but I was as Lutheran as I was Catholic. Looking back, it seems kind of silly now, considering the slight difference of opinion Luther had with the Catholic Church and the minor impact it had on Western Culture over the past 500 plus years.

Back then, it was all so boring and totally irrelevant to my daily life. My mom and dad eventually realized the Lutheran thing wasn't working, so we tried different churches until we landed at Yorba Linda Friends Christian Church. The "Friends" church is a modern-day expression of the old Quakers (yup, the ones who make oatmeal), but that's not why I liked it. The pastor at the time was John Werhaus, a former Dodgers third-baseman, but that's still not the reason I liked it.

Yorba Linda Friends was a great church because it had an awesome youth group—by which, of course, I mean there were many cute girls who were interested in hanging out with a good, wholesome (not so much) Catholic school baseball star.

I may have looked the part, but trust me, I was not the guy you wanted to see on your doorstep to pick up your daughter. I would have told you we were going to the movies or the mall, but those weren't the only destinations I had in mind. I'd spent far too much time in the locker room to be trusted. I had too much desire, too big an appetite, and too little self-control.

Yet it was at this point in my life when I met a girl whose family treated me with consideration and kindness. They saw beyond my confident exterior and glimpsed the pain and struggle I was compensating for on the field and in the classroom. They were a strong

Christian family who did their best to encourage and love me, but I was a tough sell.

I enjoyed playing the role of skeptical pessimist, especially with my girlfriend's mother. She tried to convince me of a God Who created the world, and I assaulted her with the claims of modern science. I couldn't understand how any intelligent person could believe God made the world one day at a time when brilliant minds like Charles Darwin, Stephen Hawking, and pretty much every great modern scientist assumed evolution was a proven fact.

Honestly, I thought the Bible was an interesting book, a good piece of literature, and an important historical document, but perfect and written by God? Come on. That was stuff only priests and homeschoolers believed.

No sex before marriage? I understood why that was the stance to take in public, but once the curtains were closed and the bedroom doors were locked, I was pretty sure that even the most religious teenage Christians were getting it on. Most of the ones I knew were.

My interest in psychology, moral relativism, and magic encouraged me to be highly skeptical of most expressions of Christianity. I believed it could be a really positive influence for some people, but that certainly didn't make it true for everyone.

The thinkers, philosophers, scientists, and magicians I respected were intelligent, well-read, persuasive individuals who agreed that religion had certain societal benefits but no capacity to make objective, absolute statements about the nature of reality.

The Christians I knew were nice, well meaning, but a little too simple and gullible to take seriously intellectually. My girlfriends' family saw me as a missionary opportunity, and I saw them as the closest thing to my youthful ideal family.

There was one other important dynamic in our relationship. My girlfriends' dad was a pitching coach at Loyola Marymount University—one of the schools hoping to add me to their baseball roster. It made sense. He let me date his daughter, I would be a major addition to his team, and his daughter and I would continue dating in college in the fall. I verbally committed to our little arrangement, but all those other schools didn't have to know about it. I thought, *"Why not enjoy this whole recruiting thing a little longer?"*

I was a high school senior ready to be wined and dined by some of the nation's best programs. In addition to LMU, other lucky suitors who won the right to date this hard-throwing bachelor were Pepperdine, Cal, Arizona, and the last-minute longshot, the University of Texas.

When the Longhorns reached out to me, I laughed and thought there was no way I would ever consider moving to Texas. Why would I leave Southern California?

Two words: Augie. Garrido.

♣ ♦ ♥ ♠

Augie is a coaching legend. He's the winningest coach in the history of college baseball. He's won five national titles, and he's the only coach to win a championship at two schools (Cal State Fullerton and Texas) and also the only coach to win the title in four different decades.

And Augie wanted to meet with me.

He arranged to meet my father and me at the Four Seasons in

Newport Beach, one of the most exclusive, beautiful spots in Orange County. He rocked the bling—wearing several of his massive, glittering national championship rings to impress me.

It worked.

Augie told me Texas would pay for everything, I'd get to play right away as a freshman, and joining the Longhorns was like guaranteeing my ticket to Omaha, Nebraska, and the College Baseball World Series at least once during my time in Austin.

I'd heard enough. Nothing more needed to be said. There was no decision to make—I was going to Texas. In the back of my mind, I knew I'd already verbally committed to Loyola Marymount—not just the school—I'd given my word to my girlfriend's dad.

Sitting down with him to explain I'd broken my verbal commitment and signed a letter of intent with Texas was the hardest thing I'd ever done. He was furious. He bit his lip, lowered his head, stood up, and walked away. I wish he would have screamed at me, but he didn't. His daughter and I dated for years; his family had been a huge source of encouragement during a very difficult season in my life. They loved me when I really needed it, and I repaid them by breaking my word, betraying them.

They didn't forbid me from coming over ... after everything I'd done, I was still welcome in their home. Our relationship was more than a little strained. For months, he wouldn't look me in the eye and left when I came over. I didn't blame him—I'd really let him down.

But Austin, Augie, and my fast track to the big leagues were waiting for me. I packed my bags and didn't look back.

# CHAPTER 4

---

# MAGIC ON THE MOUND

*"All pitchers are liars and crybabies."*

Yogi Berra

February 12, 1999

Baton Rouge, Louisiana

They call it "The Box"—and without a doubt, it's the most intimidating venue in all of college baseball.

Even on weekdays, the stadium overflows with rabid, screaming fans madly in love with their LSU Tigers and teeming with hate for whoever is brave (or stupid) enough to come in and face them.

Opening night is always special. The long wait of the offseason is finally over as a new season, filled with championship promise, gets underway. The atmosphere was electric—somehow, for every one of the roughly 8,000 fans in attendance, this game was personal.

The Tigers won the College World Series in both 1996 and 1997 and were heavy favorites to win for the third consecutive year before being dramatically upset the previous season. The bitter taste of that crushing disappointment still lingered. They'd waited nine long months for revenge.

It was the largest crowd ever assembled to watch a college baseball game at "The Box"—breaking a record that stood for seven years. The place was rocking, and we were in the visitors' dugout.

The drama didn't end there. We'd played LSU the year before in Austin, and they were still upset over some unusual strategy we'd employed then to ensure a win.

The game started late, so the umpires and coaches decided it would be called at a certain time, no matter what inning we were in. Armed with that understanding, we took our sweet time toward the end of the game to guarantee the win.

The Tigers hadn't forgotten.

♣ ♦ ♥ ♠

With the help of the raucous crowd, in only eight pitches, we'd made three outs. In the bottom of the first, the noise caused an error, allowing LSU's first batter to get on base. He stole second, then went to third on a wild pitch. Before we blinked, the Tigers were up 3-0.

They scored again in the second, and the bullpen got the call from the dugout to start warming up.

Pitching in this kind of atmosphere is difficult, but appearing in long relief in these circumstances is practically impossible. The starting pitcher has time to mentally prepare, to build a game plan for what to do. Confidence comes from this preparation and plan to face certain hitters.

In long relief, you're thrown to the wolves on short notice, and all the momentum is in the other team's favor. Yet you have to find a way to get batters out.

In LSU's half of the third inning, they'd already scored a run, and the bases were loaded with one out. Augie decided our pitcher was done. Tiger fans went nuts—they'd chased our starter in just the third inning, they were up 5-0, the bases were still loaded, and the game was teetering on the brink of becoming a blowout.

Augie looked down at our bullpen and motioned for me. As I jogged toward the mound to get the ball, I looked up into the crowd. This was the biggest, most intimidating environment I'd ever played in. I was going to need every trick I had to get us out of this jam.

Apparently, the fans knew who I was because they started shouting, "Marilyn!" and "FUN-ROE!!!" as the entire stadium turned to watch me. About halfway to the mound, I caught the eye of a crazy Cajun fan, holding a baby in one hand and flipping me off with the other.

I absolutely loved it. This was what I'd always wanted. This was why I'd gone to play at the University of Texas. Here was an audience of 8,000 crazy, screaming Cajuns, watching my every move. The mound was my stage, and the little white Rawlings ball with the red stitching was my magic wand.

Time for some magic.

♣ ♦ ♥ ♠

With the bases loaded, the first guy I faced was their second-baseman Blair Barbier. The following year, as the team captain, he went on to lead the Tigers to the national championship with a dramatic come-from-behind victory at the College World Series before playing professionally for the Chicago Cubs organization.

Adrenaline coursing through my veins, my heart pounding so hard I thought it was going to burst out of my chest, I felt like I could throw the ball through a brick wall.

Barbier felt it, too. He wasn't trying to make contact or put the ball in play. He swung so hard, he almost fell over. He was going for the kill shot—he wanted to take me deep for a grand slam. Luckily, he missed that first pitch and hit it foul.

On the second pitch, I got him to fly out, but a runner scored on the sacrifice fly. The next batter was their leftfielder Trey McClure—another All-American who hit 27 home runs the year before. Like Barbier, he was looking for his first long ball of the season, but I got him to pop up on the first pitch.

Poof! On just three pitches, I'd magically worked us out of the jam. I ended up pitching the last five innings, giving up just four hits and one more run—McClure finally managed to take me deep as he homered in the eighth.

The fans never let up either—they'd done their homework and proceeded to make pointed and lewd suggestions about my sister, my momma, and me.

You gotta love Southern Hospitality.

We rallied to score five runs in the top of the ninth, but came up short, losing 7-5, but Augie encouraged me and told me I did a great job under the circumstances. He said my performance helped shift the momentum. The next day, we came back and absolutely crushed them 16-4 and took the series by winning the third game 10-4.

It was only my sophomore year. I thought it would be the beginning of many memorable outings on my way to Omaha, Nebraska, the College World Series, and eventually the big leagues.

It ended up being the best performance of my baseball career.

♣ ♦ ♥ ♠

By the end of my junior year in high school, I'd committed to go to Texas and play for Augie and the Longhorns. I never second-guessed my decision to go to Austin—and once the greatest coach in college baseball history wanted me to play for him, I immediately became a much bigger deal.

I went into my last season at Servite with huge expectations.

It's one thing to pitch in front of scouts who wear polo shirts featuring the most prominent universities in the country. It's something completely different to look out and see some of the most famous logos in all of sports (the Yankees' interlocking N and Y, Red Sox nation's single white sock with the red heel). Knowing they came out to see you generates a little nervous energy.

All those long afternoons in the backyard, working hard on fundamentals with my dad, all the summers spent on travel teams, all those relaxing Saturdays (and Mondays, Tuesdays, Wednesdays, etc.) I'd given up in pursuit of my dream finally paid off.

I was bigger and threw harder than 95% of my peers. I had a commanding fastball with movement and a decent changeup. My curveball was so-so, but everyone knew you wouldn't really learn to throw a good curveball in high school because it can put too much strain on a young arm.

The important lessons had been mastered—how to strategically paint both the outside and inside corners of the plate, how to set up pitches, and most importantly, how to know exactly what to throw to get key outs in pressure situations.

This aspect of pitching is a lot like being a magician.

Greg Maddux, the first pitcher in Major League Baseball history to win four straight Cy Young Awards (the annual award given to the best pitcher in baseball) was notorious for knowing which cards his teammates held when playing poker in the clubhouse. Maddux was also famous for being elusive with the media to avoid giving away any secrets to his method.

When Greg's brother Mike (a pitching coach for the Milwaukee Brewers) was asked to explain this, he simply said, *"Magicians don't tell everyone their tricks, do they?"*

No one ever mastered the almost sixth sense a pitcher needs to be successful the way Maddux did. Like magic, it's all misdirection and sleight of hand. You become an expert at lying. The batter tries to guess what you're going to throw, and your one job is to fool him.

Successful pitchers anticipate the batter's approach and always keep the ball one step ahead of him.

The real competition between a batter and a pitcher is not physical—it's mental—which explains why most pitchers are so emotional. Catchers like the great Yogi Berra have to keep us under control, but that's their problem.

We have to let it rip. I really liked that part of it.

It's psychological warfare. Your music, your warm-up is all part of

developing that persona. You fuel your emotions in order to produce adrenaline that helps you intimidate the batter. You learn what a guy likes to hit in different situations, and then you work to constantly mix and match your pitches to keep him off-balance.

It's a lot like doing card tricks. That might be why I was good at it.

At one point and time, Baseball America ranked me as one of the Top 50 prospects in the nation. I finished my senior year with a record of 11-2 with an ERA of 2.05 and a better than 3-1 strikeout-to-walk ratio. I was routinely competing with and beating guys who were being drafted into the big leagues straight out of high school.

It was becoming clear that I would be drafted, too, but after extensive talks with Mom and Dad, I'd decided unless the offer was so astronomical I couldn't pass it up, I'd play college ball for Augie in Austin and get my degree.

As we expected, the Tampa Bay Devil Rays drafted me in a later round in 1997 after my senior season. My agent's best guess was that the earliest a team would draft me would be in the third round, and the signing bonus at that time for a rookie in that range was about 400k—an amazing amount of money for an 18-year-old—but not enough to keep me from college.

Looking back, I'm very grateful for my mom's perspective and advice. We made the right choice. Despite the years of history and the long hours of hard work put in by genuine experts, scouting kids is an inexact science, especially in baseball. Rankings and projections are mostly speculation.

Until you put a kid into pressure situations against the highest levels of competition, you have no way of knowing how he'll respond. Like the award-winning film *Moneyball* proves, conventional wisdom isn't always wise. Far too often a "can't miss" prospect ... *misses*.

In both life and baseball, sure things aren't always so sure. So many things can go wrong. A player's hype may have more to do with his personality than his talent. Pitchers often peak too soon. Lots of really talented kids can't make the jump to the next level of competition. The demands of travel, responsibility, and a grueling season are incredibly taxing and require unique maturity and temperament even the most talented athletes often lack.

♣ ♦ ♥ ♠

Augie wanted the chance to develop the potential he saw in me, but what neither of us understood, was before long, we'd discover I wasn't really that good. The problem wasn't physical—I was big and strong, had good mechanics, and competed hard.

My challenges were mental.

I was an immature kid who was deeply insecure and unsure of himself. I didn't have the mentality to be a great baseball player, but for a season and a half, I fooled my coaching staff, my teammates, and, most of all, myself.

My first appearance as a Longhorn happened in Southern California against another historic program—the USC Trojans. It was pure magic. I came on in relief, pitched two scoreless innings, struck out three, and picked up the win in front of many of my friends and family.

It was an amazing debut that looked even more impressive by the end of the season when those same Trojans won the National Championship in Omaha.

My next three games were against perennial powers Stanford, LSU, and Miami—my college career was everything I'd hoped it would be and more. I was living the dream.

A dream too good to last.

During the rest of the season, I usually came on in relief. At some point in the game, we'd get a call down in the bullpen to get up and start throwing so we could be ready to take the mound. Toward the end of the season, we were at home against Iowa State when I got the call I'd gotten so many times before. I didn't think anything of it. I grabbed my glove and a ball and stepped up on the practice mound to start loosening up with the bullpen catcher.

After a few typical pitches that I'd thrown tens of thousands of times before, I felt my shoulder pop.

Within a few hours, I learned the devastating news—a torn labrum. The labrum is the cartilage in the shoulder surrounding the socket. The shoulder socket the joint fits into is very shallow, so the labrum is incredibly susceptible to tearing after extended periods of strenuous use—like hundreds of hours of throwing a baseball.

The medical staff informed me that recovery meant rotator cuff arthroscopic surgery, a serious procedure with a long recovery time.

Don Drysdale, the great Hall of Fame pitcher for the Dodgers once said, *"A torn rotator cuff is a cancer for a pitcher, and if a pitcher gets a badly torn one, he has to face the facts—it's all over, baby."*

♣ ♦ ♥ ♠

I wasn't ready to give up. I wasn't ready for it all to be over. I was determined to outwork the injury, to throw myself into the rehab program, to lift weights like never before, to come back better than ever for my sophomore season. Our strength and conditioning coach developed a great plan, which I threw myself into with everything I had.

On paper, it was the perfect plan, and we executed it flawlessly. After starting that next season with the greatest moment of my pitching career at "The Box" in Baton Rouge, everything looked perfect. I'd bounced back from a devastating, career-threatening injury to pitch better than ever.

But it was fool's gold. An illusion. Misdirection. Don Drysdale was right.

My shoulder was done.

I wasn't ready to be done. A few weeks after the triumph against LSU, I started against UT El Paso—a fine program but not exactly college baseball's elite. I couldn't get out of the second inning.

Augie came out to the mound and said, *"It just doesn't look like you're trying today."*

I was furious.

*"I don't care what it looks like to you … I'm working my butt off out here."*

I was passionate, but I wasn't smart. My coach proceeded to weave a tapestry of profanity unlike anything I'd ever been exposed to in my life. He reminded me who was running the show as he chewed me out in front of the home crowd for a solid 25 seconds.

I learned not to talk back to him again.

My love for baseball began to wane. There was no more magic. The reality that the Major Leagues were probably no longer in my future began to set in. I was beat up emotionally from the constant pain and disappointment.

I wanted to quit.

Augie knew I was losing my passion and drive to be great. Somewhere along the way, it stopped being the game I grew up loving as a kid. Over the years, he'd witnessed this tragic process take place in so many others, and now he could see it sinking on me like a dark, black cloud.

And then, my shoulder popped again. I knew it would require another surgery. I had nothing left to give. I couldn't do it. I was told I could keep my scholarship and continue to pursue my degree despite my injury. I would receive a full ride, and my education would be fully paid for.

I decided it was time to hang up my cleats.

It was the longest walk of my life to that point. Disappointing a living legend is not something you look forward to.

I approached the greatest coach in the history of college baseball in the visitor's dugout at Disch-Falk field in street clothes as my teammates were warming up for practice. I told him I was done. I left that meeting in tears.

I didn't just leave my baseball career in the visitor's dugout that day. I left my identity. Baseball was my life. And now it was gone.

♣ ♦ ♥ ♠

The only other part of my identity was my magic. When I came to Austin in the fall of 1997, I'd continued to develop my skills as an illusionist. I loved showing up at fraternity and sorority parties; these were the easiest crowds I'd ever performed for. It doesn't take much to freak out drunk frat boys, and with a little creativity, you can blow their minds. They would absolutely lose it.

It was some of my finest work, and I'd never had more confidence as a magician.

One time I grabbed a frat boy's lit cigarette, took a big drag, held the smoke in my mouth for effect, placed the lit cigarette in my empty hand five inches from his face then blew the smoke over my hand. When I opened my hand, of course, the cigarette had supernaturally disappeared from this universe.

The guy's mouth remained unhinged for a solid three minutes.

Another time I attempted to make a sorority girl's ring disappear only for it to end up fastened on my keychain. It was an inspired idea, but in the process of the illusion, I dropped the ring in the pitch-black parking lot behind the sorority house.

I couldn't kill the trick, so I tried feverishly to convince her that the ring had genuinely disappeared. She was ticked. The only way out was to press deeper into the illusion. I couldn't find the ring anywhere, and a mass of humanity was moving through the area, stepping all over her precious ring.

After a few moments, I borrowed a bouncer's flashlight, found the ring, and made it appear in the girl's drink. She probably wouldn't have appreciated all the extra "floaties" in her drink from the parking lot and the party goers' shoes, but her mind was so blown, she didn't stop to think about it.

With baseball out of my life, these moments were all I had. I did whatever I could to keep the party going. Anything to keep my mind off everything I'd lost.

I began to drink compulsively—even for a college student. I drank away my sorrows every night and even some days. My grades slipped. I tried changing majors to create new educational intrigue and motivation, but it didn't help.

My life was spiraling out of control—which created the ideal moment for my longtime, long-distance girlfriend from back home to pull the plug on our relationship. In the back of my mind, I had always planned to marry her.

With that final blow, the last of my major life plans were smashed in a pile on my bedroom floor.

She made the right decision. I was cheating on her anyway. Bad got worse.

I barely made it through the spring semester. I decided I'd stay in Austin that summer, so I tried working for a sales company, selling books door-to-door. I quit after five weeks.

I packed my stuff and drove back to California, not knowing if I'd return to Texas because I was so beat up. I spent that summer on the couch of an old high school buddy, not wanting to face the reality of life without baseball.

To keep my mind off the mess of my life and to make ends meet, I worked at a movie theatre and delivered pizzas. It was beyond humiliating. I was supposed to be playing semi-pro baseball in Alaska and trying out for the U.S. Olympic team.

I chased away depression through constant smoking and drinking, spiraling further down the hole, ever closer to losing my grip on reality. Because I'd moved back to Orange County, I was able to see my girlfriend again to give it one more shot. I kept trying to get her to take me back, and there were moments when she let me in her life, but she could see what was happening.

I was a loser, and she knew it.

She tried to be supportive, but I reached a level of self-hatred that nobody could pull me from. I was out of answers, out of tricks.

All of my magic was gone.

# CHAPTER 5

---

# I MET TRUTH AT A STRIP MALL

*"You can only find truth with logic if you've already found truth without it."*

G.K. Chesterton

I couldn't believe it had come to this.

This nonsense was for the weak, not for me. I had clear insights into the inner workings of the human mind and the sociological constructs of culture. I'd been studying the politics of religion for years.

I was too smart to be suckered in by superstition and fairy tales. It was all a trick—and I was an expert at tricking people.

Like Marx said, religion was the sigh of the oppressed culture, the heart of a heartless world, the spirit of a spiritless situation. It was the opium of the people. It's a fantasy for poor people, a fabricated tool that helps them cope.

I was way too proud for a crutch. And I'd already promised myself I wouldn't let it come to this, but lately, I'd been breaking all my promises.

So here I was on Sunday morning, September 12, 1999, back in Austin, Texas ... walking into church.

This wasn't even a real church—it was a bunch of Jesus freaks and Bible thumpers who were meeting in a renovated strip mall.

These two dorky guys used to hang out on campus at lunchtime outside the athletes' dining hall, trying to make friends and invite people to church. It turns out my ex-girlfriend's mom had been worried about me and randomly met one of them when he was at the Anaheim Convention Center in Orange County for some weird "ministry conference."

Whatever that was.

I think she knew I was circling the drain after my baseball career ended (it wasn't a secret), so she begged him to call me, and like the good Christian he was, he followed through on his word.

After all those arguments in her kitchen, and all the time I spent challenging and questioning what she believed, the absolute last thing I wanted to do was to let my ex-girlfriend's mom win. I would never admit she was right, because then I'd have to admit I was wrong.

The only reason I showed up at church that morning was because I thought I needed my girlfriend back. Turns out, it wasn't about her—it was what she represented. Life with her was familiar, stable, safe ... and most of all, under my control.

♣ ♦ ♥ ♠

I was so angry. I hated my shoulder for breaking down.

I hated my coach for convincing me to come to Texas.

I hated my teammates for being healthy and continuing to pursue their dream while my identity was shattered in a million pieces.

I hated that all the perks that went with being a Longhorn athlete—free drinks at the club, the athletes' dining hall, an invite to every fraternity/sorority party, late-night hook-ups with random girls—were all gone.

I hated being a normal student in Austin. It was not what I signed up for. My life in Orange County was way better.

But most of all, I hated me.

If I had been stronger, this wouldn't have happened. Why did I choose to come to Texas? I should have stayed in California. Maybe if I'd honored my commitment to Loyola and my girlfriend's dad, none of this would have happened.

Whenever I stopped and thought about it, I always came to the same conclusion. It was all my fault.

I felt like such a loser.

I decided I wasn't go to cry about it and feel sorry for myself—that wasn't my style. I would forge a new identity, prove myself, and do something significant with my life.

Many young, virile college men prove their masculine significance in two critical ways: consume enough alcohol to nearly kill yourself AND hook up with as many different girls as possible. These became my passion.

An obvious place to begin this quest was at ground zero for binge drinking and continuous, casual sex ... *a fraternity house.* I rushed one of the houses, although from the beginning, being surrounded by a bunch of dudes who desperately wanted to belong felt beneath me. My "pledgemates" (*I think that's what you call them*) were way too into the whole deal. I wasn't looking for "bros" to watch *Swingers* and *Old*

*School* with while thinking up increasingly disgusting ways to insult each other. I was there for the parties.

With this attitude, I lasted one day in the process. The house threw a massive rager to kick off rush season. It was supposed to be a glimpse of what every night at the house would be like. The levels of unbridled debauchery were so spectacular, Kurt Cobain, Mick Jagger, and even Caligula himself may have been impressed.

This all seems so compelling and exciting at night when hundreds of scantily-clad coeds are wandering around, the music never stops, and you're chasing one beer after another.

No one tells you what it looks like the next morning.

On nearly every college campus in America, you can find fraternities busted for every kind of crime you can imagine, and yet, there's no shortage of incoming newbies ready to sign up and pay their dues to get in.

It's all an illusion, a magic trick—fraternity brothers are charlatans.

Our first assignment as rush pledges was to clean up the mess. "Mess" is not the right word. In the light of day, it looked like hell opened up and vomited all over the house. Every living area, bedroom, and entryway were covered with rotting trash, disgusting grime, soiled undergarments, and bodily fluids the best CSI units in the world would struggle to identify.

The "Pledge Master" who was my "bro" the night before now wanted to boss me around like a drill sergeant while I cleaned up this atrocity. I laughed in his face and quit.

I never talked to those guys again.

♣ ♦ ♥ ♠

I decided to press on with my quest to prove my alpha male masculinity. I tried hanging out with friends from classes who I'd treated as social lepers when I was on the baseball team. I was willing to party with anyone as long as there was access to copious amounts of alcohol and ladies who were looking for a good time ... or, at least, trying as hard as I was to run from their pain.

Turns out there were a lot of us out there.

During those weeks, I routinely woke up in places (and with people) without any memory or recollection of what happened the night before. My lifestyle was betraying the values my parents had instilled in me, and this realization only filled me with more shame and embarrassment, which caused me to spiral deeper down the hole. Depression and sadness completely clouded my thoughts. After looking unsuccessfully for love and fulfillment, I began to doubt whether these universally desired notions existed or if it was all some form of projection.

The school semester ended, and I was forced to make some important decisions. Losing baseball didn't just shatter my identity, it left me hungry for competition and a great challenge. I wanted a difficult task with a scoreboard where I could win.

Around that time, representatives from a company that sold books door-to-door approached me on campus and told me I could make $10,000 in sales commissions during the summer. Spontaneously, I agreed and went to Nashville for a week of training before being sent to the thriving metropolis of Kinston, North Carolina.

Not only did the "Southwestern Company" train us in the finer points of selling to complete strangers books we had never read, they also gave us a method of knocking on a door … to find a place to live.

Think about that.

You walk up to a house, ring the doorbell (if there is one), and simply say, *"Good afternoon, ma'am. My name is Jim, and I'd like to live with you. By the way, would you like to buy some books? No, I haven't read them, but they're really good. I go to college. I know what I'm talking about."*

All those years playing piano, pitching, and doing magic made me a natural. I loved to win over strangers, and I was really good at it. I would have made more than the money they promised if I'd lasted the whole summer, but after 5 weeks, I was bored, tired of small town North Carolina, and painfully tired of who I had become.

In another moment of inspiration (or insanity), I hopped in my truck and drove from the Atlantic Ocean in Jacksonville, North Carolina, to the Pacific Ocean in Orange County, California. I stopped only to fill my gas tank and empty my bladder. I consumed a non-stop diet of Red Bull and NO-DOZE and made it home in 46 hours flat.

Sometimes I wonder how I survived that trip. No one in his right mind would be stupid enough to risk his life on such a fool's errand, but I wasn't in my right mind, and I didn't value my life.

♣ ♦ ♥ ♠

My self-hatred and anger at all I'd done to destroy my life was growing stronger by the moment. I refused to stay with my parents in my current condition, so I stayed on my cousin's couch in Tustin for a few days—a city in Orange County closer to the ocean than either my mom's or my dad's.

A few days turned into the whole summer. I punished myself every night through heavy drinking. Deep down, I wanted to reach my breaking point, to hurt myself, to end the worthless mess my life had become. I sank darker and darker.

I can't imagine too many situations more depressing than what had become my home—a lumpy, dilapidated, itchy couch, reeking of sweat and beer. Forget Pier 1, this ancient piece of broken-down furniture wasn't good enough for the bottom of the ocean.

Most days I woke up (mid-morning/early afternoon) to the cracking sound of another beer being opened. The great philosopher Homer Simpson once described beer as *"... the cause of, and solution to, all of life's problems."*

Summer ended, and I managed to drag myself back to Austin for the start of my junior year at UT. It was a very difficult decision, but staying in California would be giving up and I wasn't a quitter. I went back to living with my former teammates which also meant I returned to inhuman levels of alcohol consumption and sexual depravity. As the injured, washed-up athlete, the only way for me to stand out was to party without any regard for my wellbeing.

My disillusionment with traditional morality and social conventions was being fueled by my psychology major studies. My distaste for hypocrisy and idealism led me to especially load up on philosophy and religion courses to uncover all the ways the naïve and simple had been conned through the years.

I discovered modern biblical scholarship featured the practice of textual criticism—this academic approach engages the issues most

Christians ignore—contradictions in the text, historical inaccuracies, logical fallacies, and secondary edits to original manuscripts to alter intended meaning.

One of my professors painstakingly detailed all the reasons why the Gospel accounts could not be trusted ... only to identify himself as a Christian. Finally. Someone let me behind the curtain. What I'd expected all along was true.

Christians knew a lot of their traditions were made up. If it worked for them great, but don't feed me some line about absolute truth. My professor may have been educated, polished, and successful, but he wasn't morally or spiritually superior to the guys I was working with at Circuit City.

I may not have used the exact phrases, but portions of *"Turner's Creed"* described how I felt about the world.

We believe in Marx, Freud and Darwin
We believe everything is OK
as long as you don't hurt anyone
to the best of your definition of hurt,
and to the best of your knowledge.
We believe in sex before, during, and
after marriage.
We believe in the therapy of sin.
We believe that adultery is fun.
We believe that taboos are taboo.
We believe that everything's getting better

despite evidence to the contrary.

The evidence must be investigated

And you can prove anything with evidence.

We believe there's something in horoscopes

UFO's and bent spoons.

Jesus was a good man just like Buddha,

Mohammed, and ourselves.

He was a good moral teacher though we think

His good morals were bad.

We believe that all religions are basically the same—

at least the one that we read was.

They all believe in love and goodness.

They only differ on matters of creation,

sin, heaven, hell, God, and salvation.

We believe that man is essentially good.

It's only his behavior that lets him down.

This is the fault of society.

Society is the fault of conditions.

Conditions are the fault of society.

We believe that each man must find the truth that

is right for him.

Reality will adapt accordingly.

The universe will readjust.

History will alter.

We believe that there is no absolute truth

excepting the truth

that there is no absolute truth.

We believe in the rejection of creeds,

And the flowering of individual thought.

Which brings me back to September 12, 1999.

♣ ♦ ♥ ♠

The night before I went to the weird little church in the strip mall, I was out drinking on 6th street until 2 am. I wasn't buzzed or tipsy, I was "passed-out-and-wake-up-in-Mexico" drunk. Luckily, I didn't, and somehow, I managed to pull myself together, take a quick nap, hop in the shower, and jump in my truck.

I rolled into the back of the church with my hat pulled low, wearing my sunglasses. I didn't want anyone to see my bloodshot eyes, and my hangover pounded away on the sides of my skull louder than the drum kit. The drummer, the lead singer, and the style of music were way different than anything I'd ever seen or heard in "church" before. They were African-American—this was a full-on Gospel music experience.

To say I was uncomfortable and out of my element would be a huge understatement ... and yet ... I stayed. I can't explain it. I don't understand why I didn't find a reason to bail. Something was happening, but I knew too much to let it happen. I was a master of illusion, a psych major, keenly aware of the culture and psychological triggers ministers use to captivate their audience.

But it wasn't about them. I was looking for something deeper. And suddenly, unexpectedly, miraculously, I found it.

Through the passion, the music, and the message, I experienced something new. It wasn't a feeling. It wasn't an emotion. It was more mysterious and profound. It was a supernatural connection, pulling at my heart.

My head couldn't stop this. These weren't facts that I was learning through the recesses of my mind. I don't remember what was said. In that moment, the undeniable reality of God's existence became so clear. He wasn't a series of facts to be debated or researched. Truth wasn't a set of right answers.

Truth was a person—and He and I met that morning.

I've never been the same since.

# PART TWO

The ordinary ...
becomes EXTRAORDINARY.

# CHAPTER 6

---

# NO LONGER ALONE

*"The most terrible poverty is loneliness,*
*the feeling of being unloved."*

Mother Teresa

It's a terrible thing to be alone—especially when you're constantly surrounded by people.

No matter how many people come in and out of our lives, loneliness stalks all of us. It chips away at our sense of worth as it whispers over and over, *"No one understands what you're going through ... because no one cares. No one knows who you are. And no one ever will."*

Performing in front of audiences always helped me chase away these feelings whether I was playing the piano, lip-syncing, doing magic, or playing baseball. But my parents' divorce sent me into a spiral and turned the whispers of loneliness into Dolby Digital surround sound.

Once baseball was ripped out of my life, loneliness hit me with decibel levels you could find only at LAX or a Justin Bieber concert.

My psychology professors didn't need to tell me how powerful these emotional forces can be. They were my last thoughts before I fell asleep and the first ideas to greet me the next morning. No amount of alcohol or disposable relationships chased them away.

I would do anything to silence the loneliness—that's how I ended up at a church in a strip mall. My plan was simple. Go to church, do the "God thing," convince my ex-girlfriend I was a good guy, and magically, my life would be all better again. I could be the guy I was in high school—a winner in the classroom and on the diamond, someone prestigious people pursued.

I didn't really want to go back to those days—I really wanted to silence the loneliness, the depression, and the self-hatred.

It didn't work.

♣ ♦ ♥ ♠

My old girlfriend never took me back, but someone else did. Someone who saw past my baseball hat pulled down low over my sunglasses. Someone who wasn't bothered by my blood-shot eyes or my hangover.

I'd heard about this person all my life, but we'd never truly met. Until now. This was different. I couldn't explain it. I didn't really understand it.

But I knew I'd met Jesus.

I'd experienced Him for myself—and I had absolutely no idea what to do next. The whole thing freaked me out. I was terrified this meant I was on my way to full-blown, Kool-Aid drinking, Bible-thumping, TBN-watching simpleton.

But at the same time, I couldn't deny the incredible sense that I wasn't alone after all. I was known, completely and fully, to a degree I couldn't imagine, much less articulate.

I heard people say, *"Jesus is my best friend,"* but I always thought they were weird. How do you hang out with Jesus? Do you talk to the air? Do you save a seat for Him at the movies? Do you play two-player video games by yourself and set up a controller for Him? I had no clue.

No matter how real my encounter with God felt, emotions and supernatural experience weren't enough for me. I'd spent too much time behind the curtain. I was a confidence man. A charlatan. I could convince an audience of intelligent college students that I could "float" a foot off the ground.

When people told me Jesus was the best thing that ever happened to them, I quickly dismissed it, as any intelligent person would, as an indicator of limited life experience. You simply couldn't make that claim objectively without sampling a greater percentage of everything life had to offer. And yet, I was starting to understand why they would feel this way. But feeling wasn't enough for me. I needed to research it for myself.

What really bothered me among "born-again Christians" was the lack of intellectual curiosity and integrity. Honestly, it still bothers me. It's not just the clichéd, shallow answers like *"God moves in mysterious ways," "God helps those who help themselves,"* or *"God made Adam and Eve, not Adam and Steve."*

The truth is, I'm still not over this. It annoys me on a regular basis. Most Christians refuse to engage with the honest questions atheists, skeptics, and followers of other religions wrestle with. I'm not sure if they feel guilty for asking or if they're afraid of where their questions might take them.

Either way, far too many followers of Christ haven't done the work to study, understand, and articulate what they claim to believe, and as a result, it's very difficult to take them seriously or respect them intellectually.

They may have a general, basic idea of what they're supposed to believe, but very few can tell you with any genuine insight or clarity why they believe it. I refused to live this way, so I started to put in the work. I hadn't even picked up the Bible yet—I wasn't going to spend my time diving into a several-thousand year-old collection of books until I knew I could trust it.

I devoured everything I could get my hands on.

Boxes from Amazon started showing up on my doorstep so regularly I had to go get more bookcases. The first books I read were disappointing—a popular apologetic book written by a skeptical journalist and a classic defense of the faith from the 1980s. I found both books to be overly simplistic, filled with circular reasoning, and lacking in academic credibility. I was utterly unconvinced. I needed more.

Fortunately, I discovered a brilliant thinker and writer—Ravi Zacharias—who not only articulated and engaged with the questions I was asking but fashioned incredibly nuanced, thought-provoking responses from a biblical perspective. It was thrilling—finally someone who'd encountered Jesus in a powerful way who also understood and cared about skeptics like me.

I ordered all of his books, tapes, and CDs—back then you couldn't download a year's worth of podcasts or stream content, but honestly, I'd have read his material on scrolls, papyrus, or cave walls if I'd had to. Studying and listening to Ravi led me to discover C.S. Lewis (*Mere Christianity, The Screwtape Letters, The Problem of Pain, The Great Divorce, etc.*), Francis Schaeffer (*The God Who Is There*), and G.K. Chesterton (*Orthodoxy*).

I also continued to study the other side, too—Christopher Hitchens, Richard Dawkins, Freud, Nietzsche, Marx, and even Hitler's *Mein Kampf*. When readers come over to your place, they always check out what you've got on your bookcases—whenever people saw that one, it freaked them out.

Secretly, I enjoyed their bewilderment.

While many of these writings were clearly the product of brilliant minds, they also described in detail the sobering reality of tortured souls. In different ways, each of them had given into the loneliness. They'd chosen to embrace it. The existentialists (Jean-Paul Sartre, Albert Camus, etc.) puzzled me. They were fascinated by death because it was the final curtain, the one way to discover whether or not we were truly alone in the universe.

Most magicians I've studied and met share this same deep curiosity in the back of their minds. Is there a grand design to life, an elaborate narrative being woven, or are we all alone in this cold, dark universe?

This study shaped my earliest days as a young Christian. As I threw myself deeper into study and research, I found my trust in Christ and my desire to know Him more growing on a daily basis.

However, my process was very different from all the other Christians I'd known, and as a result, I felt strange and alone. This experience was so significant and meaningful, I couldn't hold it all in. I craved dialogue and interaction.

♣ ♦ ♥ ♠

The strip mall church I'd visited was heavily involved on campus at UT, and not just by the two guys who hung out near the athletes' dining hall. Because I'd lost my most favored status and had become an ordinary member of the student body, I wasn't eating at the cool kids' table anyway. The church happened to have another campus pastor.

Morgan Stephens was different. My combination of skepticism and intellectual pride (let's call it what it was) didn't scare him. He was actually intelligent, wrestled with many of the questions I was processing, and had also played college baseball. He could see beyond my philosophical sleight of hand and all my linguistic smoke and mirrors.

Morgan is hyper-competitive, and poking holes in my ideas and arguments became like a game to him—a game he almost always won.

Part of me was genuinely excited. I'd never met anyone like Morgan, but I couldn't shake the suspicion that it was an act. I knew all too well how susceptible the human mind is to being fooled. We'd stay up late, talking through all my questions as he patiently walked me down the road into greater understanding of Who Jesus was and how God's Word applied to my life. His answers weren't trite clichés or religious crutches. There was a depth, a substance to what it told me. These ideas weren't just challenging the way I thought. I was changing.

STAYS AWAKE AT NIGHT LONGING FOR SOMETHING MORE.

HIS SKEPTICISM IS A DEFENSE MECHANISM.

SCARED OF COMMITMENT.

BELIEVES IN MIRACLES, BUT RELUCTANT TO ADMIT IT.

ARROGANT, BUT DEEPLY INSECURE.

For the first time in a long time, values like trust, hope, and joy were slowly resurfacing in my soul.

Because of my friendship with Morgan, I continued to be intrigued by this new brand of Christianity I was experiencing. I decided to give my life to follow the teachings of Jesus. I didn't have it all figured out, but I'd seen enough to know I wanted more.

Not long after, Morgan began talking about a friend who was headed back to Austin to begin an internship with the athletic ministry of the church we all attended. During those early days at the church, I was constantly meeting new people and hearing stories about all kinds of interesting characters, but this particular friend was unique.

Two things stood out about this individual: everyone who knew him couldn't stop talking about him, and he had one of the weirdest hippie names I'd ever heard.

Tennyson.

Tennyson? Who names their kid *Tennyson*? A poetry-loving mother from Boulder, Colorado, whose other two boys are *Somerset* and *Chance*.

Whenever Morgan talked about Tennyson, he'd get this funny grin on his face and start laughing like the two of them shared some inside joke. Apparently, he'd played football at the University of Colorado under Bill McCartney before a devastating injury cut his career short.

Maybe we'd have something in common after all. At least we could compare scars and sob stories.

One day after school, I went to Morgan's place like I did almost every day. He was packing his stuff because he was getting ready to move into a bigger place with Tennyson during his internship.

For some reason, Morgan thought the best solution was for Tennyson to stay on my couch until their new place was ready. We'd become close, and I trusted Morgan, so I gave a non-committal *"Sure,"* still hoping some other option would emerge before this hippie, intern, poetry-football-player showed up.

Suddenly, Morgan yells, *"T! Come in here. I want you to meet somebody."* I had no idea what I'd agreed to.

From around the corner emerged one of the largest human beings I'd ever seen. It may have been my active imagination, but it felt just like the scene in *Jurassic Park* when Jeff Goldblum's character looks into the puddle as it vibrates with each T-Rex step before the giant dinosaur bursts from the bushes.

Tennyson's massive size (6' 4", 250 lbs.) wasn't the only problem. He'd just gotten out of the shower, and he greeted me with no shirt, nurse scrub bottoms, and a towel around his neck. He looked like he'd been working out. Athletes size-up each other when they first meet, and it didn't take me long to realize he could bench press three of me.

And yet there was something genuine and disarming about him. Meeting giant, shirtless football players who're going to sleep on my couch and share my bathroom makes me more than a little uncomfortable.

But when Tennyson looked me in the eyes, smiled sincerely, and extended his hand, I stopped worrying. Like so many other times, Morgan was right. Tennyson was someone I needed to meet.

♣ ♦ ♥ ♠

The big guy with the weird name who didn't like to wear a shirt wouldn't just sleep on my couch for a couple of weeks. He would become the most important friend I'd ever had.

Tennyson and I shared much more in common than incredibly promising athletic careers cut short by major injuries. More even than the same taste in movies, quirky and unusual personalities, a mutual disgust for hypocrisy in all forms, a common commitment to pursue truth, and a growing passion to know and love God.

Turns out Tennyson had another secret. He loved magic, too. It was like we were meant to be together, like someone had decided we were destined to become friends.

I started to see traces of this grand design everywhere I looked. I never expected to go to Austin, Texas. I never prepared for life without baseball. I never planned on going to church at a strip mall. I never imagined I'd give my life to Jesus. I never knew a pastor like Morgan. And I definitely never anticipated a best friend named Tennyson.

And yet these were the most significant moments in my life. Somehow, mysteriously, supernaturally ... I was no longer alone.

# CHAPTER 7

---

# I Always Wanted a Brother

Dale: *"On the count of three, name your favorite dino-*
*saur. Don't even think about it. Just name it. Ready?*
*One, two, three."*
Dale and Brennan: *"Velociraptor."*
Brennan: *"Did we just become best friends?"*

Will Ferrell and John C. Reilly, *Step Brothers*

I never had a brother, but I always wanted one.

I loved my sister, but I always imagined a brother would be different. I always had friends growing up, but a brother was different—like
a permanent sleepover. Someone who was always there to play with,
compete with, and get into trouble with.

After awhile, I gave up on the idea. I convinced myself I would be
fine without one. But then when I least expected it, in a way I couldn't
explain, Tennyson became my brother.

He's a world-class charlatan—he's always looking like he knows
something you don't. His poker face is pretty good, and his speech
drips with so much sarcasm that unless you really know him, you're
never sure if he's messing with you.

He loves to give people nicknames, even the first time he meets you. After that, he'll never call you by your given name again. I call our friends Morgan, Eric, Brandon, and Brian, but to Tennyson, they're *Mo, E-Mo, B-Nav, and Nutties.*

It didn't take long after Tennyson started sleeping on my couch to realize why he always looked like he was up to something. He was.

♣ ♦ ♥ ♠

Most people make small talk to look for common ground. He searched for a quirk or weakness you were willing to laugh about, and he'd still be teasing you about it weeks later.

All athletes love to compete, whether they're on the field in a game, playing video games, or throwing paper into a trashcan from across the room. We lived in a constant state of competition, and Tennyson was a master manipulator.

We killed hours on the old Nintendo 64, playing "Goldeneye"— the original multi-player, first-person shooter. Four people play at the same time, running around, trying to shoot each other, kind of like a 64-bit version of paintball with a James Bond theme.

It was ridiculously competitive. We'd yell at each other, complain our controllers weren't working right or the game was flawed, but T would stay real calm.

*"Hey, Jimbo. You're the better player. You really are. Everyone knows you're the best player in this room. It would be a shame if someone as bad as me beat you. You're the best. I'm lucky to have the opportunity to play with someone as skilled as you."*

All he needed was for me to look over at him, laugh, think about a comeback and ... BANG! I'd be dead, and he'd be laughing.

For a deep-thinking, serious introvert like me, this took some getting used to. I'm reserved, somewhat private, and not a big fan of awkward moments. Tennyson enjoys embracing the awkwardness more than the writers of *The Office.*

One of his favorite moves is to follow a friend into a public restroom from a distance and wait patiently to see which stall he ends up in. There aren't too many more vulnerable situations you can find yourself in, especially in public. You'd be sitting there, handling your business as discretely as possible … when suddenly, a giant head appeared, hanging over the top of your stall.

*"What's up, Jimbo? How are things going down there?"*

Tennyson pulled this move so regularly, our friend Brian actually planned his daily routine so he and Tennyson weren't in the same spot at the same time. Tennyson never gets tired of this move—in fact, all he has to do is to think about it, and he busts up laughing.

We love the same kind of movies, and one night after watching a goofy Kevin Bacon horror movie about ghosts and people coming back from the grave, I went to the bathroom, turned off the light, and went to bed. I'd been lying there for a good three or four minutes, about to fall asleep, when I heard an unmistakable noise … a whisper.

I shot up in my bed, flipped on the light, and looked behind the doors and all around my room to see where it came from. I stuck my head out into the hallway, and nothing was there. It sounded so real, but I decided it was only my active imagination. I turned the light off, jumped back in bed, and was finally falling asleep when the whisper came again.

This time I knew. Tennyson was crouched outside my door. I had to give it to him—I was a little freaked out.

I shouted through the door, *"T! Shut up! Go to bed. I'm not scared!"*

I wasn't mad. It was actually pretty funny. But after another three minutes, as I was finally about to fall asleep, the whisper called out again.

As I laid there in the dark, wondering whether I was hearing things or whether my roommate was messing with me, a massive arm appeared from under my bed and grabbed me in the chest.

I screamed like a little girl, flew out of bed, and flipped on the lights. Tennyson was about to pee himself from laughing so hard under my bed. He'd folded himself up like a pretzel and hid under there for more than a half hour in order to freak me out.

♣ ♦ ♥ ♠

After everything I'd been through with my family, the shattered dreams of my baseball career, and my self-destructive identity crisis, Tennyson was the kind of friend I needed. He came into my life at the perfect time. It had been years since I'd laughed so hard and enjoyed everyday life the way I did with him.

I'll never forget the first time I saw *The Skittle*. A man's car, especially an athlete's car, says a lot about him. One of the ways college athletes with obvious professional careers often get into trouble is by taking money to get amazing luxury cars while they're still students.

No one ever accused Tennyson.

*The Skittle* was the name we gave his bright blue Geo Metro. It was a glorified go-kart, and in Texas, where everyone drives a truck, it looked like something you'd see at a Theme Park, not on the free-way. But he loved it. He put a racing stripe on top of the car from the front bumper over the hood, roof, and trunk, tinted out the windows, tricked out the stereo.

A Geo Metro doesn't have the sophisticated style and speed of a Mini Cooper or the convenience and efficiency of a Smart Car. It's just tiny.

He'd have to get into the car in stages, like he was playing the old board game "Twister," every time he wanted to go somewhere. It was hilarious, and instead of being self-conscious about it, he cherished every moment.

When I first met him, like most guys, I'd been a little bit skeptical and intimidated by his size and the way he looked at me. But as big as he is on the outside, he's bigger on the inside. He's always thinking of others and how he can add value to them, even when they aren't around. He loves spending time with all kinds of people, and though he never put it this way, I think turning complete strangers into friends is one of his favorite games. It's not just the challenge he enjoys—it's what the process produces.

But Tennyson is so much more than a buddy, someone easy to hang out with. He loves to talk about Jesus—not the way religious people talk about Him as *"the man upstairs," "Gentle Jesus"* hugging sheep, or a hippie-looking dude rocking Birkenstocks and a blue shawl.

He believes Jesus is still calling people to follow Him, to come home, to discover the life-changing good news of the Gospel. He tells anyone who will listen about Jesus. He's the kind of guy who goes to

Dairy Queen to grab a blizzard, and by the time he leaves, he's praying with the kid behind the counter who wants to give his life to Christ.

Tennyson is serious about the integrity of his faith. It's not a crutch, not a moral blueprint to help you live a better life or to be a good person. He'd wrestled with all the same questions I'd been working through, and the process caused him to love and respect Jesus and His early followers so much more.

Some of the other people at my church didn't understand my questions and couldn't figure out why I couldn't take things on blind faith, but Tennyson didn't rush me. He let me work it out. He listened and helped me process, but there was never any pressure to prove myself.

♣ ♦ ♥ ♠

Whether it was my issue or someone else's, I felt that pressure constantly. The church community I joined was dynamic, passionate, diverse, and filled with big personalities. There were moments I felt like it was the place I'd been looking for my whole life, and then there were times I was convinced it wouldn't last.

Deep down I worried I wasn't like these people, and sooner or later, they would all find out.

No one knew about my love for magic. I hadn't been a Christian long, but I was fairly certain it was against the rules. Even if it wasn't, I was sure it wouldn't help me to feel more connected to this new group of believers.

I didn't know what to do about it. Magic had been part of my life for so long, and I was afraid I'd be forced to give it up if anyone discovered my secret.

I waited patiently for the topic to come up, so I could observe how everyone reacted before I admitted anything. And once again, Tennyson came through for me.

The day after Morgan introduced us at his apartment, we'd all been invited to a houseboat party on Lake Travis in Austin. There were 40 or 50 of us on this beautiful boat, and when we walked down into the kitchen, I saw a small group of guys. One of them had a deck of cards and was doing some really basic tricks—so simple that a small child could do them with a little practice.

I was so certain because I'd done them back in junior high.

Immediately, I began to wrestle in my mind—part of me worried about fitting in, but the other part longed to perform and blow their minds. Before I could make a decision, I noticed someone else had joined in with them. Tennyson had the deck of cards, and before long, jaws were dropping, and people were shouting.

Tennyson was into magic, too.

After he finished, I gave the growing crowd 15 minutes of some of my better tricks—intricate and nuanced illusions I'd been honing and perfecting for years. A few of the Christians thought I was the devil, but Tennyson thought I was the man. I didn't care what anyone else thought—I wanted T to see what I could do.

When the party was over, we went back home and talked about magic the way teenage girls talk about boy bands.

We couldn't get the words out fast enough and stayed up most of the night comparing notes. His father was an amateur magician who studied some of the greats—Dai Vernon, Charlie Miller, and

Jean Huggard. I showed him the stacks of magic books I'd collected over the years.

During the long talk of illusion, magic, and wonder, we both realized the greatest mystery of the evening was how we found one another. We both were recovering from the loss of certain professional athletic careers due to unexpected, devastating injuries. We both were uncertain about our futures but were growing in our desire to know and serve Jesus with our lives. We both shared a passionate interest in mystery, illusion, and the supernatural. And now astonishingly, inexplicably, we were roommates.

Sometime in the early morning hours, long after midnight, we made a commitment to each other. We were going to do something different; we were going to invite people to search for truth and explore the wonder of a relationship with Jesus through mystery, illusion, and magic.

♣ ♦ ♥ ♠

In the Summer of 2000, *NAILS MAGIC* was born. We chose the name because we wanted to be edgy and sharp; we wanted our audience to be pierced deeply with the truth.

Subtle, right? We didn't care.

We wanted to preach the Gospel to the world through the power and mystery of our illusions. It sounded better in our minds than when we told somebody else.

In hindsight, it probably wasn't the best choice. It's kind of a strange name. Maybe we should have realized we were missing our target demo after all kinds of nail salon ads and free subscriptions to manicuring magazines showed up at our house.

We didn't care if people didn't get it. We were so convinced of the genius of our idea, we knew it was only a matter of time before everyone else came around and recognized our brilliance.

In 1997, David Blaine debuted a one-hour special on the ABC Network called *Street Magic*. David is a strange dude who intentionally developed an unusual persona—his off-putting, pained, and mysterious manner created the appearance he was cooperating with darker, unseen powers.

It was genius.

One of the most important things about the special was the way the camera focused as much on the reactions of the people in the crowd as the trick itself. This heightened both the intrigue and the drama of what he was doing.

Penn Jillette called Blaine's Street Magic *"... the biggest breakthrough in our lifetime"* and *"... the best TV magic special ever made."* We loved those specials, and yet, as we watched them, we realized the two of us could do every trick he was performing. All we needed was an audience. The special reawakened the public's interest in magic and made it cool again. We soon learned we could draw massive crowds in almost any public setting.

Tennyson and I could walk up to anyone on a college campus, act strange as we did a few tricks, and all of a sudden, we'd be surrounded by a huge group of people who were freaking out and calling their friends.

Over and over, people said, *"These guys are like David Blaine! Can you levitate, too?"*

The magic came easier to me, but Tennyson could draw a crowd without any magic. He loved meeting strangers and talking with anybody, and people are naturally drawn to him. Before long, we realized we had the potential to do something really significant.

♣ ♦ ♥ ♠

We had a talent that could generate relationships and build rapport with total strangers.

We had a story to share.

We had a powerful, life-changing message to communicate, but we had no idea how to transition from doing street magic to preaching the Gospel.

There was another challenge as well. Most of our illusions were close-up tricks that wouldn't translate to an auditorium or a larger venue. Our ever-expanding library of magic books and materials were filled with instructions and techniques for illusions traditionally performed by Harry Houdini and other legends.

But those kinds of shows required elaborate props and grand venues ... and lots of cash. Cash we didn't have.

At this point, two surprising things happened. First, one of the pastors at our church who'd played professional basketball for the Houston Rockets had been praying about us and decided to invest $5000 as seed money for our new start-up.

We were blown away.

Unfortunately, we were just as surprised to discover how many Christians (many in our church) were offended by our idea that magic and illusions could be used to honor God and tell people about Jesus.

It seemed so obvious to us, but we were being criticized ... and they'd never even seen what we were doing!

While this discouragement and criticism stung, we weren't about to give up. Tennyson and I were convinced this wasn't simply a cool idea or a fun new hobby. We genuinely believed God called us to do it. He'd been working in our lives, preparing us for this moment; only He could tell us to stop.

This conviction we shared kept us going through a lot of difficult moments in those early days.

♣ ♦ ♥ ♠

The two of us were convinced we were supposed to do this, but we didn't really understand what "this" was. What we needed was a mentor, a Yoda, a Mister Miyagi who could train two young Jedis in the ways of the Force.

Our search led us to Lubbock, Texas, where we met with the president of FCM—the *Fellowship of Christian Magicians.* Neither one of us knew there was an FCM, I still don't know how many people are in it, but we'll never forget the first one we met.

Rick Honea pastored a church and did stage shows on the side. He liked to be called "Preach," and our new mentor agreed to help us adapt a version of Houdini's famous *Sub Trunk* illusion. One person would go into a large wooden crate while the second person would handcuff, shackle, and place his partner into a bag before locking and chaining the entire crate. Then the second person would stand on top of the crate as a large curtain was raised completely over them. Moments later, when the curtain dropped, the first person would have been "substituted" for his partner—putting the "Sub" in "Sub Trunk."

Preach suggested the illusion to us, and immediately, we saw ourselves performing the feat in front of a massive audience glued to our every move. However, there was a "small" problem—most magicians are slight, and Tennyson and I are both big boys. Preach wasn't worried about it—we'd just have to build huge crates.

Preach and his family were so generous and accommodating to a couple of former college athletes so obsessed with magic they stayed up 24 hours straight building a Sub Trunk in a small country church. Once we finally finished building the monstrous contraption, we rehearsed over and over until it became muscle memory we could perform with little effort or strain.

In addition to the Sub Trunk, I made a walking cane dance around the stage. I carefully swallowed a few razorblades and string before pulling them both out of my mouth at the same time. And we did this telepathy bit where Tennyson walked through the crowd to find personal items (credit cards, driver's licenses, pictures, money, etc.) from the audience while I described them in detail without seeing them.

Our act wasn't Vegas-ready, but it wasn't terrible either.

We started touring churches in the Austin area. Everyone agreed our performance was entertaining, but we could tell most people were skeptical to the idea that anything significant would ever come of it. They did everything but pat us on the head while telling us in the most patronizing, elementary-school teacher voice, *"Isn't that sweet? You both did soooooo good."*

Some humored us, some didn't get it, and some thought we were nuts.

But we knew we were on the verge of something huge. Our athletic backgrounds taught us the great things we could accomplish through practice and hard work, and we were more than willing to put in the work. Tennyson and I started to attend large magic conferences in Vegas and Orlando.

Watching Penn and Teller perform together in Vegas was a defining moment for us—not only because they were a two-man team, but also because they made no apologies about flat-out preaching a message. Penn is militant and aggressive with his atheism—his book *God, No!* and his podcast, *Penn's Sunday School*, are persuasive, agenda-driven preaching wrapped in pop cultural trappings.

In those conferences, we became sponges, soaking up as many ideas, tricks, possibilities, and tools for presenting as we could to use in our own show. We brought home as many books as we could fit in our luggage. Tennyson's ability to draw crowds and befriend strangers wasn't only entertaining in this context—it created a huge opportunity to network.

As only he could, T managed to make his way to both David Blaine and Penn. Penn wasn't interested in small talk or hanging out, but when T passed David Blaine a note with his phone number and the simple phrase, *"Take a Chance,"* we were pleasantly surprised when our favorite street performer decided to call us.

The hard work, commitment, and vision for what we were doing started to pay off. Slowly, gradually we built a great reputation. Not only were we making an impact in the greater Austin area (and throughout Texas), but we were starting to have opportunities to travel as well.

A series of shows on several campuses in Nashville were huge successes. In Los Angeles, we intentionally botched a *bullet catch* after we secretly prearranged to end the show with a shooting accident. We even left the event in a real ambulance.

Our shows in Atlanta at prestigious historically black colleges and universities like Spellman and Morehouse were wildly popular. We later learned our shows were the second largest events ever held at these incredible universities. The only person who drew a bigger crowd was Bill Cosby.

Second to Cliff Huxtable himself? Not bad for a couple of goofy white guys.

♣ ♦ ♥ ♠

In a short amount of time, we'd gone from dreaming all night about our future the second day we met to creating and developing a successful traveling magic ministry. It was awesome. We booked as many dates in as many different places and settings as we possibly could.

During this time, two drastically different events helped me understand at a deeper level the supernatural significance of what we were doing.

I didn't forget for one moment we were performers ... *illusionists ... magicians.* Our show did not feature mystical powers, but the people who came to our shows lived in a world bigger than they could explain or understand purely through reason or logic. They already knew the world was filled with mystery—and so did we.

Our show may have been a series of tricks—sleight of hand, misdirection, and carefully crafted wording to create the illusion of supernatural power. But there was nothing fraudulent about the God Who sent us.

We may have been charlatans, but our God was genuine.

We wrestled with this tension. Tennyson and I liked the influence magic provided for us, but we weren't giving our lives to it. We wanted to make a difference in the lives of people. We wanted those who were lost and hurting to find the same Truth, the same Person, Who had transformed us.

One night after a show for a youth group in Lago Vista, Texas (about 20 miles outside of Austin), Tennyson and I drove home in separate cars. We'd left really late because we'd stayed after the show to talk and pray with several teenagers who were struggling with cocaine addiction.

I was driving my black Ford F-150 (my father bought it as a reward for earning a college scholarship) along the windy roads hugging the hills overlooking a massive valley and steep ravine on the way back to Austin. Our whole show was in the back of my truck (the Sub Trunk, lights, speakers, mics, etc.) when a drunk driver slammed into a car in front of me at more than 65 mph. I struck both cars, pinning my truck against the railing overlooking the ravine, and I was pinned against my airbags.

I had to crawl out the passenger window, and when I did, I saw my truck was totaled. Even more unnerving was the realization it was teetering over a ravine at least a hundred feet deep.

The drunk driver who started this pile-up was motionless inside his car, so I yelled in to try to help him. There was no answer. He'd died in the crash. The driver of the other vehicle couldn't walk for years.

The doctor asked me if I'd seen M. Night Shyamalan's *Unbreakable* because he couldn't understand how I walked away with only a few scratches. He called it absolutely miraculous.

He was right.

I knew God's hand protected and rescued me from death that night. My story wasn't finished.

I didn't know where my story was going, but I had a growing sense it was far more significant than even my greatest dreams of baseball glory.

This wasn't a game—this could change lives.

Not long after I first gave my life to Christ, a man walked up to me at church and told me he'd been praying for me, and in that moment in his mind, he saw a picture of me on a beach at one of the most southern parts of Australia. He said I was crying my eyes out.

It was so random. He seemed like a nice guy, total weirdo, but nice guy nonetheless.

Nine months later, my church planned a missions trip to Australia—an interesting coincidence, nothing more. I had no money to go running off to Australia ... until someone paid for my trip. Getting weirder, but the trip was in August, which happens to be the middle of winter down under.

Tennyson went, too, and we did some shows at the University of Melbourne. Yes, Melbourne is in Australia, but it's not in the south, so my prayer friend must have heard wrong. But during one of our shows, we met a student who was a surfer, who enjoyed the show so much, he asked if we could spend some time with him the next day. We agreed, and he picked us up really early, so he could drive us two and half hours south.

As our new friend parked the car, I got out and realized I was standing in the exact spot where the man told me I would be. I needed some time to myself. I snuck off to the side, and I lost it. I was bawling—loud, ugly, slobbering tears. God knew how skeptical and untrusting I could be, and yet, in that one moment, He communicated so clearly how much control He had over my life.

No matter how much I doubted, His power and plans would overcome my skepticism. I didn't realize it then, but this became a recurring theme in my life.

A businessman from Orange County heard about what we were doing and believed so strongly in our vision, he raised $100,000 for us and connected us to the largest campus ministry organization in the world.

The God I never fully trusted had given me the brother I'd always wanted. And He'd given the two of us a platform to do something great.

# CHAPTER 8

---

# COME TO AUSTIN INSTEAD

> *"Don't get me wrong. I love the ladies.*
> *I mean they really rev my engines."*
>
> Paul Rudd as Brian Fantana, *Anchorman*

Once I became a Christian, I worked really hard not to be noticed by the ladies.

It was the best strategy I knew to distance myself from the guy I used to be—the con-man, the sex-crazed athlete, the ladies' man, the playa.

I hated that guy ... he was a giant d-bag.

These deeply imbedded character flaws don't change over-night—they have to be completely re-wired from the inside out. I knew I was the problem, but I also hadn't spent much time in healthy relational environments.

No gentleman, no man you'd want spending quality time with your daughter goes to baseball clubhouses or frat houses to learn how to respect women.

For the first time, I was regularly observing how a man of integrity views and values women. Both Tennyson and Morgan demonstrated what this looked like and began to coach me to follow this biblical pattern.

It was like learning to walk all over again.

All the years of performing, pitching, magic, and psychology had given me an innate advantage with not only the fairer sex but everybody I interacted with. Whenever I met someone, I immediately searched for an advantage—an insight, an interest, a physical feature, an obscure detail—I could call upon to help accomplish my agenda.

Now I was learning to willingly set all those advantages aside in order to take on a posture of honesty and humility, to put the needs of others above my own, to engage genuinely and vulnerably in authentic relationships.

Let me be clear—I've still not mastered this by any means. In fact, every day I realize how much more I need to grow in these areas as I continue to follow Christ.

But I'd never seen ANYONE even attempt to live this way. It definitely took some time for this way of life to become my new normal. My attitude and expectations were being radically confronted and changed on an ongoing basis.

It seemed to come natural to Tennyson; it was simply everyday life to him. He listened closely, watched for and noted nonverbal communication, and was emotionally available for people.

In his mind, it wasn't a strategy for getting ahead in life, for winning friends and influencing people—it was the best way he knew to practically apply Jesus' command to love others.

Unfortunately, most people aren't used to being treated this way. Especially ladies.

Morgan and I used to laugh at how many girls thought Tennyson was into them because of the respect and attention he freely offered. They thought he was getting ready to give them flowers and ask them out when instead, he was moving on to show the same care to the next person he talked with.

It didn't come quite so easy for me.

♣ ♦ ♥ ♠

I'd always loved the attention I received flirting. The process carried all the same risks and rewards of performing. *Oooh. Look at her. Can I get her to laugh, smile, give me her number? Yes. Yes, I can.*

Giving it up was really difficult, but I knew it wasn't Morgan or Tennyson asking me to change. The One after me was higher up the food chain. Changing my behavior or my character to please some religious authority figure felt dishonest and dirty.

But changing to please the God Who had rescued me wasn't an option. I wasn't going to stop until I was a different man.

The sovereignty of God—the belief He is in control of all of history, from the fate of nations to the individual details of each of our lives—was, and is, an incredibly intriguing and challenging concept. Part of me is repulsed by it while another side of me longs and hopes it's true at the deepest levels.

When it came to my sexuality, my future spouse, and the family I hoped and prayed for, I whole-heartedly embraced the idea that God knew what I needed better than I did.

My history with the ladies made it clear I was either self-destructive or an idiot ... or most likely ... *a self-destructive idiot.*

Left to my own devices, I worried I'd choose the wrong girl, we'd start down the family road, and the whole thing would implode, shattering the lives of everybody involved—the pattern I'd observed in my own life and the lives of so many others.

I made the choice to trust God to bring the perfect person at the perfect time, and the best way I could demonstrate this trust was to honor and treat all women with respect.

After Tennyson dropped in my life like a bomb, school became an afterthought. It was there in the background, but I'd decided when I was done, I would pursue a career in both magic and ministry. This meant internships, training, and becoming an employee of a Christian missionary organization.

Not exactly a career path I'd ever envisioned for myself, but it sounded doable. If T could do it, I knew I'd be able to cope as well. It was a means to an end; a vehicle.

About a year earlier, he'd spent six months in Southern California for ministry training, and in the summer of 2002, it was my turn. I wasn't worried about it. I was a SoCal kid. I'd knock out the training, do a little seminary work at Fuller in Pasadena, see some old friends, maybe visit Disneyland, and then return to Austin with the respect and admiration of my peers.

Arriving at the training school in Torrance, California, I was greeted by roughly forty other young people who I'd spend the next six months with. They came from across the country, from different cities representing all kinds of campus ministries—from large, public commuter schools to small, elite private institutions, from historically black colleges to the local campuses in the greater Los Angeles area (USC, UCLA, and Long Beach State).

We were a diverse group—athletes, international students, a few married couples—all committed to the same mission and purpose: we wanted to reach college students with the life-changing message of the Gospel.

It's always a calculated risk to bring together attractive, young, single leaders who share common values. This subject was addressed multiple times during our orientation. The school leaders told us several different ways, *"You're not here to find a spouse. You're here to be trained for ministry. You don't even need to pray about it. If the Lord wants to do something, He can wait six months."*

In the moment, it felt like overkill, but once the formal portion of our meeting was over and people started hanging out, it made sense. Looking around, I saw small clues indicating the warning had fallen on deaf ears.

The ladies were more discrete—gathered in small groups, greeting each other with warm, friendly smiles and a hug, but you could tell they were sneaking a peek, stealing a glance at the guys milling around.

The guys weren't nearly as subtle. They were laughing too loud, trying too hard, and, of course, working the room with the old Christian, opposite-sex standard: *the side-saddle hug.*

It's a classic youth group peacocking move. Frontal physical contact is too much (at least in public), so modesty dictated you throw an arm around the shoulder and squeeze. I always thought it was weird, but I guess you take what you can get.

Scanning the room, I saw a large group of guys gathered around one particular young lady. Initially, curiosity piqued my interest. I wasn't curious for long—I knew exactly what those other dudes were up to.

♣ ♦ ♥ ♠

She was 5'10", athletic, with striking features and an olive complexion. Every one of those guys was doing what they could to make an impression. I moved past the crowd, extended my hand, and introduced myself. Sticking to my commitment to stop flirting didn't mean I should be cold or standoffish.

Her name was Eli, a little unusual. The only Eli I knew was the priest in the Bible who took care of Samuel, but I didn't care. I was ready to get to know Eli better. We would see a lot of each other the next six months.

Over the next couple days, I learned a few more things about her. She actually was a model and a state track champion in high school. When we went out on campus to do ministry, it was clear she was also a gifted evangelist. Without even talking to the other guys, I knew some were praying and begging God to put in a good word with her for them.

My thoughts returned to Morgan and Tennyson and the way they treated ladies, but even more importantly, I remembered how God challenged my flirtatious ways. I genuinely wanted to honor my commitment. But seriously ... I was struggling. I was crushing hard.

I tried to go the big brother route—you know, pick on her, start arguments. One day in class, I told her she had feet like a grandmother.

Another time, during group study, she broke for some boba tea. She asked if I wanted some, certainly a kind gesture the other guys would have appreciated. When she brought it back, I took a sip. It was nasty. Disgusting. I barely kept it down. The other guys would have lied and said they loved it, but I was honest.

Depending on how you look at it, either my approach worked perfectly, or it was a total failure. Somehow we kept finding ourselves studying together or carpooling on ministry trips or swing-dancing for an hour. Okay ... that last one was probably over the line.

It certainly caught the attention of the school's leadership. I was called in and given a stern talking to. My supervisors wanted to know if they'd failed to make the standards and expectations clear or if I'd chosen to ignore them.

The bottom line was clear—either I kept my distance from Eli, or I wasn't going to make it through the full six months of training.

None of this was part of my plan. I didn't come to Los Angeles to find love, but at the same time, I didn't like being strong-armed. Yes, technically we'd disregarded the instructions, but we weren't the only ones, and we hadn't done anything unbiblical. At best it was a grey area.

Being sent home early would jeopardize my opportunity to do magic and ministry with Tennyson, so I decided to do my best to fall in line. But it was awful.

Eli immediately became distant and cold. I thought she hated me. I didn't realize she'd been given the same ultimatum.

My feelings didn't care what my supervisors told me—they had no intention of slowing down.

Eli was the total package. She was so laid back and cool, but at the same time, she was spontaneous and lived in the moment. She genuinely loved the Lord and effortlessly talked about Him with strangers. When I found out she loved Neil Diamond, too, the issue was settled in my mind.

Why couldn't everybody see *we were made for each other?*

A few years earlier, she'd left the University of Tulsa and moved to Los Angeles to pursue a career in acting and modeling. Unlike so many others, she got an agent and started working within a few weeks of landing in Hollywood. She became good friends with some high-profile actors and was quickly ushered into a world so many young people long to be a part of.

And yet, she was largely unimpressed. The veneer of fame and a showbiz lifestyle wasn't overly appealing to her. Not because she didn't have opportunities in Hollywood, but because she felt called to something more.

During our six months in Los Angeles, she went to the red carpet premiere of a movie she was in, and later, we all went together to see her on the big screen. More than 40 interns were technically training for the same job as campus missionaries, but only one of us was in a movie.

As difficult as it was, we managed to satisfy our supervisors' expectations and finished our training. I was heading back to Austin, and Eli was returning to Dallas with plans to come back to Los Angeles to work for a season sometime down the road.

♣ ♦ ♥ ♠

I'd been counting down the days until we could spend time together again, but as we were leaving, we were told it probably wasn't a good idea. I genuinely appreciated that our supervisors cared about us and wanted the best for our future, but this was too much. We'd done everything they'd asked.

To this day, I think they crossed a boundary. Yes, it was clear to everyone we wanted to be friends with the hope of something more, but that's not sin—we weren't doing anything wrong.

Back in Austin, I took some time to pray and think about it while working alongside Morgan and Tennyson. The feelings didn't go away. I talked with an older couple in the church who'd worked with college students for years. I trusted them deeply and was shocked when they told me to call Eli.

My heart raced as I dialed her number. I hadn't felt that way since the first time I asked a girl to a dance in elementary school. Eli answered the phone, and I could tell she was really excited I'd called. It was awesome.

But then she dropped a bomb. She was packed, and the moving truck was on its way to load her stuff for Los Angeles.

Before I had time to think it through and stop myself, I heard the words come out of my mouth as I said, *"Don't move to California. Come to Austin instead and see if there's something between us."*

Pure desperation.

It was out there, and I couldn't take it back. Like John Cusack in *Say Anything*, I was standing on her lawn, holding the stereo over my head. But it wasn't Peter Gabriel's *"In Your Eyes"* playing in my heart.

It could only be Neil Diamond.

*Hello again hello.*
*Just called to say, hello.*
*I couldn't sleep at all tonight*
*And I know it's late, but I couldn't wait.*
*Hello, my friend, hello.*

She said, "Yes." I couldn't believe it. We'd been on the phone for hours, and it was one or two in the morning—no chance I was going to sleep. Around 5 a.m., I hopped in my car and drove to Dallas. We spent the day hanging out. It was everything I hoped it would be and more.

I was falling for her. Actually, I was already gone.

She never made it to Los Angeles, which created some political tension between the ministry headquarters in California and our team in Austin. It was awkward and weird and seemed kind of stupid, but I didn't care.

The girl of my dreams was back in my life.

We worked on campus with each other, talked for hours over coffee, made dinner together, and went on long walks. As great as our feelings were, our love was bigger than puppy love or butterflies. We're both opinionated, competitive, and strong-willed.

Together we discovered how critical forgiveness and sacrifice are to love. Without them, you can't have love. And without love, there's no chance for a healthy, long-term relationship.

Love's not magic—you have to work at it. You have to choose love every day. You have to put the other person's needs ahead of your own, over and over and over again.

It didn't take long for me to realize what to do next.

In July of 2003 in a limousine outside our favorite restaurant in Austin, I asked Eli to marry me. I gave her a plastic, gold ring, costing a quarter in the grocery store, and she wore it on her finger. She loved it. We laughed, and when she took it off, I passed my hand over it, revealing the most expensive and precious ring I could afford.

After she said "Yes," we rode around in that limo, celebrating by sipping champagne and sticking our heads out the sunroof, laughing and singing. The evening was pure magic.

December 6th of that year, we were married at Riverbend Church in Austin and celebrated the event at the Trois Estate in the Austin Hill country, the famous setting from the movie *Spy Kids.* We still love watching that movie together as a family—not because we're huge Antonio Banderas fans, but because the kids think it's amazing to see on TV where Mom and Dad were married.

In a little more than a year, I'd met the woman of my dreams, walked away from our friendship, called her in desperation, convinced her to marry me, and said "I do" in front of our closest friends and family.

This wasn't one of my illusions. It wasn't a trick.

Left to myself, armed only with my charm, my looks, and my understanding of the way human beings work, I never could have pulled it off. Trusting God for my spouse was absolutely one of the best decisions I'd ever made.

God blessed me with the most beautiful and amazing woman

I'd ever met. It was a mystery beyond anything I could have accomplished. He supernaturally brought us through a series of challenging circumstances and questions regarding our future.

He was only warming up.

# CHAPTER 9

---

# PEAKS AND VALLEYS

Lloyd: *"We gotta get out of this town!"*
Harry: *"Oh yeah, and go where? Where are we gonna go?"*
Lloyd: *"I'll tell you where. Someplace warm. A place where the beer flows like wine. Where beautiful women instinctively flock like the salmon of Capistrano.
I'm talking about a place called Aspen."*
Jim Carrey and Jeff Daniels, *Dumb and Dumber*

People use all kinds of expressions to describe falling in love.

It may start with a crush or puppy love, then you fall madly and deeply in love until you're head over heels. At this point, some say your head is in the clouds while your feet don't touch the ground.

There's nothing like it, but it tends to make you lose track of other things going on in your life. I think this has always been true. Maybe it explains why, in the Bible, the Israelites sent a married couple away from everyone else for the first year.

Eli and I aren't Jewish, but we were definitely in love—the kind where everything makes you laugh, and you don't really care what you're doing as long as you're with each other.

I'd been so focused on Eli, I failed to really see what was going on around me.

When I first came back from the training in Los Angeles, Tennyson wasn't his usual self. He asked for, and was given, a short sabbatical from ministry.

I knew something was wrong, but with everything I was working through, Tennyson didn't make things about him. Even if I brought it up and insisted how badly I wanted to know what he was wrestling with, he wouldn't tell me.

The Tennyson I'd known was the life of the party, ensuring everyone was included, and going out of his way to make others feel valued. Now he seemed awkward, slipping slowly into the background until he was little more than a silent, somber figure on the edge of the room.

He was so genuinely happy for Eli and me. He was like family—the brother I'd always wanted. I was so honored to have him stand with me on my wedding day. The morning of the big day, Tennyson walked right into the edge of the giant bookcase next to his bedroom door, opening a gash requiring stitches on the bridge of his nose.

So weird—Tennyson was a great athlete, and the bookcase hadn't moved. He said in the morning light, the bookcase looked like the doorway, which wouldn't have made any sense had I not been in love and about to get married.

After we got back from our honeymoon and settled into our new lives, Tennyson scaled way back from his day-to-day responsibilities in the church and with the campus ministry. The one thing he was insistent on continuing was our magic.

♣ ♦ ♥ ♠

When he was on the road, meeting new people, doing tricks, and telling newfound friends about Jesus, the old Tennyson, the guy I knew and loved, was right there with me like nothing was wrong.

The late nights studying, the conferences with other magicians, and the long hours of hard work were starting to pay off. Our street magic was world-class, and even our stage show was getting better. Every day, new opportunities all across the country were offered to us.

These opportunities made us rethink our approach. NAILS MAGIC was direct, piercing, and confrontational. The magic was a set up to what really mattered—preaching the Gospel. It was never our intent to mislead anyone, but at times, some of our audience got upset and felt betrayed.

They loved our magic, but they didn't care for our Jesus. I still cringe at some of the early articles about our show in college newspapers. It felt like a bait and switch, even though we gave the audience a chance to leave before presenting our beliefs.

One thing we loved most about magic was how it created common ground with people who saw the world so differently than we did. It provided rapport with atheists and people who didn't know one Christian, and we were determined not to chase away this group.

This understanding started us reshaping and rethinking what we did in order to create more interaction, more subtle questions, and less take-it-or-leave-it calls to repentance. We were growing, definitely still under construction.

Trying to build something new is messy. And sometimes hilarious.

Our show was filled with illusions requiring audience participation. Sometimes a volunteer who seemed genuinely excited from her seat turned out to be more than a little inebriated once on stage.

Drunk girls struggle to follow directions which makes them terrible volunteers but exceptional candidates for blooper reels and outtakes.

High schools can be equally difficult. At a crazy school in Long Beach, no matter what we did, the kids refused to calm down. I told them the number one cause of death among students was alcohol-related incidents. Instead of sobering them, this fact incited hoots and shouts of *"Yeah, baby!"*

Then I informed them of the staggering number of sexually active teens who contract incurable STDs. After an overpowering roar from the crowd in response to the phrase "sexually active," we decided to call it a day.

Churches didn't always go so smoothly either.

We were performing at this cool church in downtown Nashville that met in a converted Planet Hollywood. It had multiple stories, decorative glass, spiral staircases, and people everywhere. For our grand finale, we planned to duplicate our infamous bullet catch, until the Senior Pastor found out and shut us down midway through the stunt.

Being treated this way by an older minister reawakened the mistrust and skepticism I'd experienced at the Los Angeles training. I hated that feeling. The last time I'd felt it was when I told the Senior Pastor at the Austin church that I wanted to ask Eli to marry me.

He was a charismatic leader who'd been incredibly successful ministering to high-profile athletes. Confident in his abilities, he enjoyed confronting people and expected tremendous loyalty and commitment from those he was leading. Because of these factors, he intimidated nearly everyone.

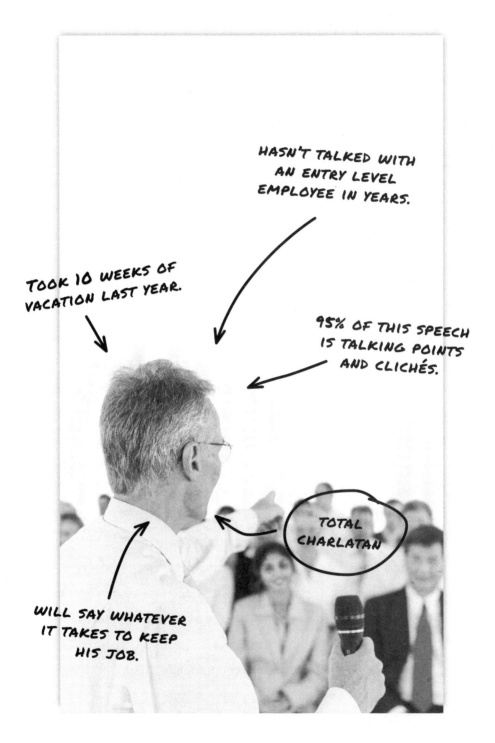

When I told him my plans, he said it was a mistake. He didn't think we were right for each other and felt so strongly about it, he refused to perform the ceremony or lead us through pre-marital counseling.

I was hurt, and every feeling of mistrust and betrayal from my past came rushing back.

Fortunately, not everyone shared his harsh assessment. Another pastor in the church who played linebacker for four years in the NFL told me he and his wife would be happy to work with us. Their love and encouragement made a great impact on us and helped us successfully walk through this important season.

Less than two years later, we all learned that our intimidating Senior Pastor, who didn't approve of our relationship, wasn't faithful in his. Unfortunately, he was the tragic crooked preacher cliché—he'd been having an affair with his secretary and mishandling finances in both the church and the athletic ministry.

This troubling discovery came in the wake of a similar bombshell involving one of the leaders in the Los Angeles training school who had been especially vocal in his disapproval of my relationship with Eli.

I was irate. I felt betrayed. I felt like an idiot. I felt like all my greatest fears about Christians and ministers were true all along.

The only hope I could hold onto was what I'd seen God do through Tennyson and me. I'd been there. I'd experienced it myself. I didn't know about anybody else, but I knew what He'd done through us was real.

♣ ♦ ♥ ♠

Discovering the existence of a counterfeit or a fraud isn't the same as disproving the reality of the genuine article.

The man who wanders through the desert being fooled by a mirage may not have water in the moment. But it does not mean water is not out there somewhere—he just doesn't have any.

Unsure what to do, Tennyson, Eli, and I prayed, asking God to show us. It turns out, the pastor who married us was planning to start a church in Denver, Colorado.

Immediately, Tennyson was going. No brainer. This was his hometown. He was beyond excited. And my heart remained fully invested in what God was doing through our magic. I was ready to join Tennyson, and thankfully, Eli was also ready for a fresh start.

In the fall of 2004, we moved to Broomfield, Colorado, a suburb of Denver and Boulder. It was a combination church plant in the city and a campus ministry at the University of Colorado, Tennyson's alma mater.

Eli and I found a great apartment behind the Flatirons Mall, located exactly halfway between Boulder and Denver. On the third-story, our balcony patio perfectly framed the beautiful Flatiron Mountains—the gorgeous beginning of the Rocky Mountains.

It was truly a fresh beginning for us ... we were pregnant with our first child and so thrilled to start our family.

Planting a church is a massive project, even for a team of people, and we also worked long hours building momentum on campus. It wasn't easy. Boulder's campus is beautiful, but the students were unlike any place we'd been before.

More than 1000 students gathered April 20th every year to smoke weed together on campus. The majority of the student body was either Birkenstock-wearing, pot-growing, dreadlock-weaving, hemp-threading pluralists who rejected the Gospel for its exclusivity or intellectual elites who doubted and mocked the historical claims of Christianity.

Even with Tennyson's connections, we had a difficult time generating interest and reaching students.

During those first few months, we put our magic show on the backburner. I started feeling real strongly that it was time for a new direction. We desperately needed a new brand to more clearly define the vision of our unique ministry.

Tennyson wasn't so sure. He was concerned about the time and energy it would take to get our show to the next level. He didn't want to wake up one day as an entertainer in Vegas, wondering how this became his life. I didn't want it either, but I knew God had given us unique skills and passions for a reason, and there was more for us than what we'd done to this point.

It wasn't time to end, but it was time for a change.

Colorado Springs, located about 70 miles south of Denver, is a hub for many Christian ministries and missions organizations. The Elevation Group—a full-service marketing, consulting, business management firm for nonprofits and ministries—agreed to help us re-brand our ministry.

We trusted The Elevation Group because it was led by two retired executives from *Compassion International*, one of the most respected ministry nonprofits in the world. We were determined to take as long as necessary to get it right and ended up taking five months to complete the process.

Choosing a name is so difficult because your name creates the first impression, shapes the organization's image, and is one of the most important pieces in building your brand. It had to be mysterious and filled with intrigue without being gimmicky.

The moment the word "MAZE" came out of my mouth, the search was over. I was convinced. A maze invites you in, it's experiential, it's puzzling, it's difficult to navigate, and while it's filled with many paths, there's only one true solution.

Filled with a new rush of excitement and possibility, we jumped into developing a brand-new portfolio of promotional materials—a logo, new photos, a website, video clips, and fundraising materials for groups wanting to hire us.

I remember driving to downtown Denver at 3 a.m. one morning for a photo shoot of shadows and darkness set against the backdrop of empty streets. The full moon in the freezing cold created an amazing effect against our black suits without any Photoshop or image manipulation.

It was a turning point for us. Everything we'd done had shaped us as artists. We weren't guessing anymore. We knew exactly what we were looking for and the images we wanted to convey.

With the re-brand, our stunning new promotional materials, and the clearest focus we'd ever had, we believed everything was ready for us to break out and become a huge hit.

We were wrong.

♣ ♦ ♥ ♠

As clear and compelling as MAZE was to us, the public didn't feel the same way. Audiences struggled to engage with us the way we'd hoped. Instead of filling them with wonder and a hunger for deeper spiritual truth, most of them either argued about the existence of God or left confused.

This was a big problem. While we'd been retooling our show and developing MAZE, Eli had given birth to our daughter in April of 2005. Once MAZE was ready for launch, we hit the road hard, pressing to get traction and build it into everything we knew it could be.

By August of 2006, we'd added a son to our family. What can I say? We were madly in love, and it turns out my wife is a fertile Myrtle.

I was home for only two weeks after Gavin was born before I went out on the road again. Probably not the wisest choice at the time, but we were desperate to get MAZE up and running. Eli believed in what we were doing, but I didn't fully grasp the strain she was under. For the first time in our marriage, a serious, future-threatening tension crept in.

Finally, in the spring of 2006, we got the break we needed.

We got a call from Ron Luce, the head of *Teen Mania*, a high-profile, international student ministry organization. Ron was looking for something different for his *Acquire the Fire* arena tour where thousands of students gathered in big venues for a night of music, creative acts, and a message.

Like everybody else, Ron remembered meeting and immediately liking Tennyson at a previous ministry event. In one moment, everything changed.

We went from performing for a few hundred people to an audience of several thousand in places like The Target Center in Minneapolis and Rupp Arena in Lexington, Kentucky. These were massive arenas, home to professional and elite college sports teams.

Along the way, two things became clear—we weren't interested in merely entertaining big crowds. The venues would never get any bigger, but our motivation stayed the same—we wanted to challenge people to engage with the truth. We also discovered it was possible to do close-up magic on stage accessible enough for thousands of people to experience and enjoy from their seats.

This meant we didn't have to worry as much about developing more stage illusions like the Sub Trunk we'd messed up so many times. It's a good thing, too, because we'd already decided we'd never rock glitter suits and jungle cats like the original famous magic duo.

With a little creativity and inspiration, we found all kinds of interesting ways to perform our interactive, crowd-participation tricks on a larger scale without losing any of the impact. It was amazing.

The good news was MAZE immediately connected with the students. We performed in every city on the ATF tour. This was also the bad news. The tour was split into two teams (red/blue), and because we were young and hungry and there was no one else like us, we worked both sides of the country at the same time.

We'd fly from Denver to Pittsburgh on Friday, wake up early and fly to Tacoma, Washington, on Saturday, then home to Denver for a day or two before hitting the road again. At the same time, we still had responsibilities on campus in Boulder.

We performed in 40 different cities in seven months.

After all the struggles, the doubters in church, and our own anxieties about our future, this kind of demand created a huge adrenaline rush and stroked our egos. It wasn't healthy.

Eli couldn't keep up the pace of caring for two babies without me most of the month. If our roles were reversed, I wouldn't have lasted a month. We talked it through and prayed about what mattered most to our family, deciding if this was our calling, she needed to be closer to her family for their support. In the summer of 2007, we moved to Colleyville, Texas (a suburb between Dallas and Fort Worth).

This wasn't just a massive strain on my family. Tennyson was crashing, too—much harder and much more regularly than I ever imagined. The difference was, he never told me.

# CHAPTER 10

---

# STRAIGHT TO VOICEMAIL

*"This is Tennyson McCarty with MAZE Ministries, and you've reached my voicemail. Go ahead and leave a message, and I will get back to you ... But just remember, things in life may seem impossible, but with God, all things are possible. Have a great day."*

Tennyson's Voicemail Message

The moments before I go onstage with MAZE are critical, similar to warming up in the bullpen before running out to the mound. I try to get my head right. I go over the show in my mind. I think about my transitions, what I want to say, how I'm going to make it unique for this specific audience.

Sometimes I listen to music. Sometimes I just close my eyes and quiet my thoughts. The absolute last thing I want to do is make small talk or answer my phone. But for some reason, in the green room at the University of Wisconsin-Green Bay, I took the call from my friend Brian.

I didn't know it, but the next 60 seconds would change everything.

*"What's up, Brian?"* I answered.

*"Jim, do you have a minute,"* he said, his voice quivering with emotion.

Immediately, I knew this wasn't a normal conversation. Brian had been with Tennyson and me from the early days in Austin. He knew our routine and wouldn't have bothered me if it weren't important.

*"Yeah ... what's going on?"* I replied as curiosity and anxiety began spiking in my gut. I had no idea what was wrong, but it was getting scarier with each passing moment.

I waited through a long, excruciating pause as Brian struggled, laboring to figure out exactly what to say. Finally, the words stumbled out through a shaky voice desperately fighting to hold off the tears. *"Tennyson is missing. We've had to file a police report."*

I felt like I'd been hit in the gut with a sledgehammer. I doubled-over, kneeling on the floor.

Brian's words picked up speed.

*"The local police usually wait between 48 and 72 hours to actually do anything when it comes to 'missing persons' reports, so we're going to begin searching for him ourselves."*

All I could manage were two words, screamed into the receiver. *"WHAT?!? Missing???"*

♣ ♦ ♥ ♠

The Acquire the Fire tour transformed MAZE magic in the seven months we zigzagged across the country. On one hand, it was everything we'd hoped, prayed, and waited for—massive, passionate crowds responding to both our show and our message. Yet the toll from the constant travel was more than we could handle.

Our success with *Teen Mania*, a predominantly high-school ministry, led to a series of bookings with Campus Crusade for Christ, the largest college campus ministry, well-known around the world. Things weren't going to slow down—the fall held more bookings in more new venues than ever before.

Eli had made it clear we couldn't continue raising two small children with my hectic travel schedule while helping with a church plant in a new city thousands of miles from family. But now that we'd settled into our new Texas home close to her parents' support and help, I was ready to get back out on the road.

The stress and strain of our schedule wasn't just my issue—Tennyson had been dealing with his own unique set of challenges. When he reluctantly took his ministry sabbatical in Austin, we all thought it was the result of pushing too hard for too long—he was exhausted and stressed. Nothing more.

It turned out things weren't quite so simple.

Tennyson eventually went to a doctor, and in 2005, was diagnosed with bipolar disorder. Like every other obstacle he encountered, T went right at it—determined to face it and beat it head on.

Standard procedure with this condition calls for strong medication to stabilize the individual's moods. He hated the medication because he felt it calmed him so much, he couldn't feel anything. He wasn't himself. He knew others could see it, which bothered him more than anything else. The last thing he ever wanted was to be a burden or a strain on other people.

Tennyson pressed deeper into God. He read every book on healing he could find, constantly quoted Scripture passages related to miraculous healing, and prayed, asking God to take away the pain.

Despite the challenges and struggles he was facing in his own life, he continued giving hope and encouragement to others without ever acknowledging or complaining about his own situation. It was amazing.

On many, many nights in our hotel rooms during the tour, he'd toss and turn in bed, unable to find the peace and rest he needed to fall asleep. I worried about him, but he had a way of putting people at ease. His big physique and bigger heart for people made him seem indestructible, but I could tell he was hurting.

Tennyson wasn't comfortable in the role of needing care. He wanted to be the one encouraging, giving, and ministering to others.

I imagined our move to Texas was tough on him, but he refused to allow me to feel bad for him. Far more concerned with Eli and the kids getting what they needed, T never put his interests above theirs.

He was determined to get off the medicine because it affected his ability to emotionally engage in relationships. After a period of intense prayer and aggressive steps toward healing, Tennyson believed he'd received the breakthrough he needed.

He went off the meds ... and for a while, he was his old self again. He laughed more, smiled more, listened more closely, and became his incredibly emotionally intuitive self. It was amazing. He couldn't wait to get back on the road for all the events Campus Crusade had lined up for us.

But then he started to crash. The awkwardness, the social anxiety, and the depression came back stronger than ever.

Finally, the Monday before the series of shows in Wisconsin, Tennyson called and told me simply in the most somber, subdued tone I'd ever heard from him, *"I can't go."*

I didn't know what to do. Campus Crusade was a critically important relationship, and we were just starting out with them. I hated to cancel the week of the event, but I'd never done a show by myself. I asked our board for guidance, and they suggested I try to do the show on my own.

So on Wednesday night, October 17, 2007, I was alone in Green Bay, Wisconsin, while the only brother I'd ever known was in Boulder, Colorado.

♣ ♦ ♥ ♠

By the time I got off the call with Brian, my mind was spinning out of control. One moment it was convincing me all the logical explanations for Tennyson's disappearance in an attempt to assure me everything would be fine.

And then I remembered the last time we talked, Tennyson's words were very brief, and I remembered him saying he was trusting God, he needed a break, and he was going to rest in the love of God.

I poured over those words with all the newfound urgency of the situation, and for a moment, my mind jumped to some terrible conclusions. Before lingering any longer in the worst-case scenario, I called Eli. Trying to contain my emotions enough to communicate clearly what was happening, I heard what sounded like my son crying and my wife screaming. And then her phone went dead.

At this point, everything seemed utterly surreal—a terrible dream I hoped wasn't real as my subconscious mind struggled to wake up. Fortunately, I didn't have time to dwell on the well-being of the people I loved most who were thousands of miles away—students were pouring into the venue, and show time quickly approached.

Most of the shark attack stories are similar. Typically, the victim is in peaceful, shallow water, totally oblivious to the lethal threat lurking beneath him. Once he realizes he's been attacked, he goes into an instinctual, adrenaline-fueled shock that lets him endure in a kind of autopilot mode. Only later, after he calms down, does the magnitude of the event hit him.

That's how I made it through the show that night.

Immediately afterward, I checked my voicemail, desperately looking for answers. My mother-in-law called, explaining Eli had been out walking when I called. In the brief moments we spoke, our one-year-old son flipped out of the stroller, hit his face on the sidewalk, and popped out his only two teeth. The combination of his bloody injury and the news of Tennyson's disappearance gave Eli an anxiety attack, and she was now recovering in the hospital.

The most important people in my life were all in serious pain while I was thousands of miles away.

I don't remember sleeping that night. Taking the first flight to DFW in the morning, I picked up my family and flew to Denver. Being with Eli and the kids created much peace for all of us as we turned our attention to helping Tennyson.

There's a stretch of toll road connecting Denver's airport to the base of the Colorado Rockies where Boulder is located. Tennyson and I had made the drive several times a week over the past year as MAZE took off. Making the trip without him, not knowing where he was or whether or not he was safe, was eerie and unsettling.

I tried Tennyson's cell—it went straight to voicemail.

♣ ♦ ♥ ♠

Brian grew up with Tennyson in Boulder, and he and his wife, Marchelle, had become our great friends from the earliest days of the church plant. Being with people we loved who could relate to what we were experiencing was comforting and gave me peace to focus my energy and attention into the search efforts.

Not long after we'd arrived, Brian pulled me aside and told me about a series of hand-written journals they'd discovered on Tennyson's bedroom nightstand. In his own words, it was clear his struggles with his bipolar condition were far worse than he'd ever communicated. He was in agonizing, desperate pain ... misery and trauma serious enough to cause someone to take drastic action.

Brian and I both had seen the strength of Tennyson's character and his perseverance through hardship. We were deeply troubled but remained hopeful.

Early Friday morning, Brian and I drove to Tennyson's house. When he moved back in 2004, he'd remodeled the home he grew up in—a beautifully rustic house perched over a rushing creek, nestled into a hillside with a gorgeous view of the Rocky Mountains. The home was over 100 years old, located in the city's first subdivision, conveniently placed between Tennyson's two schools—Boulder High School and the University of Colorado.

From the moment he'd moved back, the home had been filled continually with students, friends, laughter, and the signs of life that accompanied Tennyson everywhere he went. It was strange to be in his home without him, under these tragic circumstances.

The kitchen had been converted into command central, complete with huge maps of Boulder's roads and hiking trails, marked with red pins signifying places of interest and clues regarding Tennyson's whereabouts. Notes, legal pads, journals, laptops, videotapes, cell phones, insurance information, phone records, bank receipts, and anything else possibly containing hidden insights were scattered all over the kitchen.

It was immediately clear Tennyson's loved ones were going to do whatever it took to find him. I was filled with a fresh rush of hope and adrenaline. We were going to find him. It was only a matter of time.

Conrad McCarty, the second oldest of Tennyson's four siblings, was intently focused on his call with the Boulder police. Tennyson had now been missing for four days and three nights with Boulder temperatures in October regularly dipping below freezing. His car had not been found, and when dialed, his phone went straight to voicemail.

Conrad is an accountant, and signs of his attention to detail and brilliant analytical mind were seen all over the kitchen. He was calm and poised, but his glossy red eyes made it clear he hadn't slept much. He stressed the need to find when and where our brother had gone off the grid and asked me to crack bank accounts, credit cards, email, and health insurance in the hopes of finding any activity pointing to a location.

Tennyson's last activity was a Monday purchase at a convenience store near CU's campus, so Conrad sent one of his younger brothers, Somerset, to the store for the security camera footage. A desperate move, but we didn't know what else to do.

I tried Tennyson's cell—it went straight to voicemail.

♣ ♦ ♥ ♠

Deep down, we all waited for him to pull up the drive way and laugh at us for freaking out and launching an all-out search committee from his kitchen.

We called Tennyson's psychiatrist, hoping she might have an insight or a piece of information to help us in our search. After several hours, we learned she hadn't seen him in months, but he'd left a message a few days earlier to schedule an appointment.

Our minds racing, we continually tried redirecting our worst fears to more positive outcomes—*He was hiking somewhere; he checked himself into a hospital; he went on vacation.* Anything that allowed him to come back to us.

Sometime that afternoon, Somerset pulled up to the house in his Jeep with a copy of the security tape, but there were four days' worth of footage to search through to find images of his brother on Monday afternoon.

I couldn't sit around, doing nothing. I grabbed a friend, and we drove around the neighborhood, looking for Tennyson's silver Toyota 4-Runner, an exercise in futility and frustration. Over and over, we pulled up to a silver 4-Runner with hope and excitement, only to discover it wasn't his. Boulder is filled with silver 4-Runners, but no matter where we looked, we couldn't find the only one that mattered.

I tried Tennyson's cell—it went straight to voicemail.

After hours of searching, we finally gave up. My body was hungry, but I had no appetite. Tennyson would've been upset with me. I could almost hear him saying, *"Jimbo, go get something to eat. You can look for me later."*

Back at Tennyson's house, we discovered our search party and support group had grown considerably.

I tried Tennyson's cell again—it went straight to voicemail.

Our timing was perfect. We walked through the door at the precise moment Somerset discovered the precious seconds of security footage. No one moved or dared to breathe as he rewound the tape. The screen flickered as the feed cut between camera angles, but we clearly saw the silver 4-Runner pull up to the curb and Tennyson's lower body exit the car.

We all gasped.

The camera angle switched to the empty store, then back to the parking lot. He was standing outside his car, talking on the phone. The camera switched back to the store, but the next time it returned to our brother, the phone call was over.

After four inexplicably long days, we finally saw Tennyson. He was in the most terrible shape any of us had ever seen.

We all wanted to reach through the screen, grab him, pull him out, help him, rescue him ... anything to express how much we cared for him in that moment.

Dressed in his familiar Denver Nuggets warm-up suit, he wandered aimlessly down the aisles like a zombie. Even in the grainy footage, we saw large black bags under his eyes. His normally groomed hair was disheveled and matted.

He wandered through the store until he stopped to grab a bottle of orange juice and a pack of donuts. He never ate donuts—years of football training made him meticulous about his diet. He staggered up to the counter, paid with his MasterCard, and walked out the door.

What appeared to be a meaningless, insignificant exchange couldn't have been more urgent. It was the moment Tennyson dropped off the grid.

I tried Tennyson's cell—it went straight to voicemail.

♣ ♦ ♥ ♠

Conrad called the Boulder police detective he'd been working with to fill him in on the details of Tennyson's last known appearance. The influx of new details and some visual confirmation of Tennyson's activities gave all of us a boost. It wasn't great news, but it was something we could build on. It was progress.

Throughout the course of the day, I'd wrestled with fear and anxiety, but I'd been able to hold on to a measure of peace in my soul, urging me to keep believing everything would be okay. Tennyson was a man of faith and character and the most genuine follower of Christ I knew. Surely God would protect him, bless us as we searched for him, and cause all things to work for good in this difficult situation.

While I encouraged myself, my family needed some encouragement of their own. Brian's wife called to say Eli was having a difficult time dealing with everything—I heard her crying in the background. I drove back to meet them at Brian's house.

Eli's a strong woman, but her adrenaline wore out as the weight of everything she'd been through over the last few days finally caught up with her. Thankfully, our kids were mostly oblivious to everything happening around them, and the severity of what their parents were dealing with slipped past them. I picked up my son, held him close, and, for a moment, wished I could trade places with him.

My phone interrupted my sweet distraction. It was Bryan Schwartz, the pastor of the Boulder church we planted with Tennyson. He called to say there was a prayer meeting at his house in an hour or so. After getting Eli and the kids settled, I made the short drive to the prayer meeting. The cars lined up and down the street were a clear indicator of how many people cared about Tennyson and wanted to help.

As I made my way into the house, the first person I saw was Tennyson's girlfriend Tracy. They'd met at a show we did in Boise and immediately hit it off. She was the only serious girlfriend he'd had the entire time I knew him. Their whole family had flown in from Idaho, wanting to be close and do whatever they could to help.

Tracy looked nothing like herself—there were no traces of her customary smile or contagious, joyful exuberance. She looked like she hadn't slept in days and had spent the time crying and worrying.

The prayer meeting took place downstairs, but Tracy couldn't go—her shock and pain were too intense for her to be around so many caring but unknown faces. I stayed with her, hoping somehow to comfort and encourage each other. We shared stories, cried, and even laughed a little about how we'd pay Tennyson back for worrying and freaking us out.

After a while, the prayer meeting concluded, and people made their way upstairs. A quiet resolve, a humble confidence filled the air. As they'd prayed, they were all filled with the sense that God was in control, and He was protecting and providing for Tennyson at that very moment.

Bolstered by this fresh wave of faith and optimism, I tried Tennyson's phone again.

For the first time in days … the phone *rang*. It didn't go straight to voicemail.

At first, I was stunned. My mind raced—it makes perfect sense. He's been out of range in the mountains where calls can't go through, and now he's back in town in a coverage area.

In seconds, I'd finally hear his voice.

One ring.

*Pick up. Pick up.*

Two rings.

*Pick up. PICK! UP!*

Three rings.

*C'mon T … pick up THE PHONE!*

Four rings.

And then I heard his voice. *"This is Tennyson McCarty with MAZE Ministries, and you've reached my voicemail. Go ahead and leave a message, and I will get back to you … But just remember, things in your life may seem impossible, but with God, all things are possible. Have a great day."*

My stomach was in knots. I didn't have butterflies … more like condors or eagles were flying circles on my insides. Shaking, I was frustrated and angry, but at least I got through. It was a small step, but it was progress.

My phone started beeping—the battery was about to die. I went to the kitchen, plugged it in, and stopped at the bathroom. I looked in the mirror—I was a wreck. I washed my face, steadied myself, and went back out to hear there was a phone call waiting for me.

I saw the number on the screen—it was Conrad. My heart raced with excitement, anticipating good news. First Tennyson's phone came back, and now he had to be waiting for us at his house.

I should have been prepared for what I was about to hear. I wasn't.

*"He's gone, Jim. Tennyson's dead. A state trooper found his car."*

I must have misheard him. It had to be a mistake. In stunned disbelief, I pulled the phone closer and asked Conrad, *"Wait ... did you just say he's dead? Tennyson's DEAD?!?"*

Conrad clearly replied, *"Yes. We need you to come to the house as soon as you can."*

I still can't remember exactly what happened next. I fell to the floor in combined anguish and rage, sobbing uncontrollably and yelling from the deepest part of my guts. From the corner of my eye, I saw Tracy burst onto the front porch, vomit, and collapse into her mother's arms.

Somerset and Bryan Schwartz came to my side on the floor and tried to console me, but I was crying so hard I had trouble breathing. I didn't care. My violent yelling shook the whole house as I desperately cried, *"NO! NO! NO!"*

In my yelling, I hoped to wake myself up from this terrible, horrific nightmare. But nothing changed. It was real. Tennyson McCarthy, my partner, my brother, was gone.

I gathered myself enough to call Eli, struggling to speak the unthinkable. Our worst fears had been confirmed. I barely remember most of the next few moments. I struggled to make critical phone calls to family and close friends. Eli pulled up in the driveway and embraced me—her eyes were red and her cheeks were more swollen than I'd ever seen them. I wanted to see her before I left for Tennyson's house and faced the police who were waiting for us.

♣ ♦ ♥ ♠

Walking into his home was torturous. Everywhere were reminders, fresh ghosts of moments we would never get back or do over. Tennyson's father, his brothers, and Brian sat around the table with the officers, waiting to hear the mysterious details—something, anything to explain how this happened.

Tennyson's 4-Runner was spotted by a local fire department volunteer on a stretch of mountain road several miles outside of Boulder. Through the forest and down a hidden riverbed was a serene, beautiful vista known as "Peaceful Valley."

Tennyson's body was found partially submerged in the frigid, rushing waters of the mountain stream. The cold temperatures made it difficult to determine how long he'd been there.

I believe after doing everything he knew to do, Tennyson found this quiet, peaceful place and begged God to come take him home. From everything I could tell, it appears that is exactly what happened.

We thanked the officers for their hard work and their thoughtful consideration in answering our questions as we stood, joined hands, and prayed together. Tears fell on my hands as equal parts pain and supernatural comfort surrounded all of us gathered in loving memory of our son, brother, and friend.

♣ ♦ ♥ ♠

A week later, the McCarty family held a private funeral for 50 of Tennyson's closest friends and family in another of his favorite spots, the Flatiron mountain range overlooking Boulder. It had been Tennyson's most frequent hiking spot, a beautiful natural amphitheater where picturesque mountain views mingled with puffy white clouds as far as your eyes could see.

On that beautiful, unseasonably warm autumn day, a gust of wind caught his ashes and gently lifted him upward as we all said goodbye. It was the perfect tribute to the man who'd given his life to do the same for everyone he ever met.

Several days later, more than 1500 friends packed Mackey Auditorium at the University of Colorado to celebrate the life of a young man who'd made the most of every day. Friends, students, teammates, coaches, and teachers came together to laugh, cheer, cry, and say goodbye to a man who'd given so much of himself to his community.

Eli and I cherished the afternoon and wished our brother could have seen how deeply and incredibly he was loved.

It was unforgettable. I had no idea what to do next.

# CHAPTER 11

---

# THE FALSE BOTTOM

*"Every man must do two things alone;*
*he must do his own believing and his own dying."*
Martin Luther

*"A friend who dies, is something of you who dies."*
Gustave Flaubert

Someone once said, "Time heals all wounds," but I don't believe it. Some wounds actually hurt more with time.

I still miss Tennyson. I still don't understand why it happened. I've replayed those scenes from October 2007 over and over in my mind every few days since the world buckled on its axis.

- *What if I'd recognized the obvious symptoms sooner?*
- *What if I hadn't moved my family to Texas and stayed in Colorado? Could we have helped him receive the care he needed to save his life?*
- *What if I'd heard the pain in his voice more clearly when he called to tell me he couldn't go? Instead of being with students in Wisconsin, I could have been with my one true brother in his greatest moment of need.*

I hoped the questions, the pain, the guilt would fade as time passed. They haven't.

I wasn't the only one to blame. Where was God in all this? How could He let this happen—to Tennyson of all people? Why weren't his prayers answered? God could have healed my hurting friend at any moment, and He chose not to.

Why?

WHY?!?

I was confused, angry, and puzzled. The pain wasn't all I was dealing with.

Every doubt, every justifiable skepticism I'd ever wrestled with sprung back to life, returning to torment me.

- *You gave your life to Jesus, and what did it get you?*
- *Your friend died because God did nothing. That's the thanks you get for going into the ministry and giving your life to serve Him.*
- *You're an idiot, and your "God" is a joke.*
- *Christianity is a crutch. Or a fairy tale. It's for the weak and the dumb.*

Deep down, I didn't believe these thoughts, but I didn't always have the strength to chase them away.

After the beautiful, moving funeral at the base of the mountains and the massive, goose bump-inducing celebration at Macky Auditorium, I crashed. I felt dead on the inside.

Part of me wanted to carry on the vision of MAZE in Tennyson's memory, but another part of me couldn't fathom carrying on without him. It was too painful.

If I chose to keep doing magic, every trick, every illusion, every time I stood on a stage in front of students—the giant, gaping hole in my heart from Tennyson's absence would be ripped open all over again.

Before we headed back to Texas to try moving on with our lives, I took the present I'd made for Tennyson before his 30th birthday. It was one of our first NAILS MAGIC promotional posters from the earliest days of our show. I enlarged the image, had my whole family sign it for T, then wrote him a note where I called him my one true brother.

That poster still hangs in my house today.

When we moved to Texas less than a year earlier, we'd made a great connection with a new church family, and they were an amazing support through this process. When they heard what happened, two pastors from Gateway Church flew up to be with us at Tennyson's memorial because they knew how much it meant to us. They were right—having them with us during this incredibly difficult moment communicated a level of love and support we desperately needed.

After we returned home, Eli and I left our kids with her parents and went to Hawaii in an effort to start the healing process. The beautiful, relaxing environment provided a much-needed distraction, but even the beauty of Hawaii couldn't change how I felt about magic.

I hated it.

I couldn't be around it. I decided never to do another show. How could I? Tennyson was the gifted communicator, the more passionate follower of Christ, the one who always made the transition from magic to message. I was the performer, the expert who took care of all the show's technical details.

My ultimate responsibility was to make him look good enough as an illusionist to capture the attention of the audience during the important close of the show—when he helped people think about eternity, the supernatural, and God's plan for their lives.

I had no desire to go back to MAZE—and even if I had the desire, I didn't have the manpower needed to properly execute the show.

In my heart, I'd resolved this part of my life died with Tennyson.

♣ ♦ ♥ ♠

Several months later, I was invited to do a show for high school students in our community. I had no desire to do the show, but one of my pastors challenged me not to dismiss it so quickly. He thought it was worth considering. Out of my gratitude and appreciation for all he'd done for our family, I prayed about it.

If you're anything like me, occasionally you've prayed a very brief, general prayer with more escape clauses than a Hollywood marriage. The idea is to honor your commitment to pray but to do so in a way that ensures God would never answer your prayer.

I've learned from experience this doesn't work. Before I even finished praying, God gave me a little nudge. I knew He wanted me to do the show.

What had been described as a small show for a few high school students turned out to be a crowd of more than 800 people, including many adults—parents of students and business professionals.

I was more than a little freaked out.

The choice to obey and do the show was another defining moment—not only for MAZE magic but for me personally. At the show, I met Zak, a young Muslim high school student. He didn't care for my message, but he loved my magic. He stayed late ... long after we cleaned up the materials from the show—he wanted to talk with me.

After discussing magic, he asked if we could hang out again. Then he asked for a ride home. I said, "Yes" to both, and before long, not only did Zak become a great friend, he also became a follower of Christ.

Reflecting on the one show I agreed to do, I'm stunned to see what God was up to. My primary motivation was to obey God, but I also hoped to give someone else a glimpse of the awe and wonder I'd lost. It's always been what I loved most about magic.

In the end, it was me and not merely the audience who ended up captivated by awe and wonder. God did something beyond what I could have imagined.

He resurrected MAZE magic.

The show was more than a way to honor my brother Tennyson, my old partner—it was also the moment I found my new one. During the show, when choosing volunteers to help me, I had no idea God selected the young man who would end up working with me fulltime.

Zak wasn't the only one impressed by the show—a TV producer from a long-running, highly-respected Christian program was also there, and he booked me for an upcoming episode.

Things began to fall into place. Without even trying, I ran into all kinds of people with unusual resources who asked if they could help me. Campus Crusade was thrilled to have me back, and my calendar quickly filled.

At a summer camp in Arkansas, I met a guy who runs an organization designed to develop ministries. He helped us build a new website, shoot new promo materials, and improve our show.

MAZE was back. The quality of the show had never been better, the audiences were larger and even more engaged, and the street magic generated the most dramatic responses we'd ever seen.

It was incredible—and I knew I couldn't take the credit.

I'd been angry with God, disappointed, upset, and confused, but He never gave up on me. He remained faithful, He honored His Word, and He continued to move in powerful ways. Tennyson's dreams and hard work had not died with him—they continued to live on and make an eternal difference in the lives of young people.

He would have been so proud.

♣ ♦ ♥ ♠

One year after Tennyson died, in the fall of 2008, I felt a sharp pain in my right leg behind my knee. A few years earlier, I'd discovered a blood clot in my leg—nothing too serious—but it put me on bed rest for a few days until it cleared up. This new pain was located in the same area, but it was more intense.

The doctor agreed with my blood clot assessment and prescribed some blood thinning medication. Spending more than a handful of hours flying every week didn't help the healing process. My legs swelled on the plane and wouldn't go down until I got flat on my back and elevated them.

All my tricks and techniques barely managed the situation, let alone solved it. The pain got worse. After flying home from a historic show at the University of Maine in Bangor, the pain was crippling. Eight to ten Advil barely took the edge off. I limped off the plane, dragged my luggage from baggage claim, and hobbled to my truck. It took every ounce of strength to push down the gas pedal. Getting home was a minor miracle.

I walked in the house, threw down my stuff, and collapsed on the bed in tears. Eli took me to the ER to figure out what was going on. I was frustrated because we'd overcome so much to get to this place.

Our family was healthy again, enjoying life in Texas, and making the adjustments necessary for me to do what God called me to do.

Eli and I had worked through the unimaginable loss of Tennyson, many of the doubts and the pain it stirred on our insides, and returned to a place of confidence and peace in the goodness of God.

MAZE magic had been completely dead—and yet now, it was back, bigger and more compelling than ever before.

We'd overcome too much to let some blood clots stop us. As the doctors went in and out of the room with serious urgency, stopping in the hallway to speak in hushed, sober tones, a thought entered my mind for the first time.

*What if it's not a blood clot, but something much, much worse?*

In the wake of Tennyson's death, I'd spent almost no time thinking about my own death. That was about to change.

From then on, death was all I thought about.

# PART THREE

The grand illusion ...
which has been hidden ...
is finally revealed.

GREG & SAMANTHA

CHIP

PRINCETON

JUSTIN BIEBER

THRILLER/MJ

# CHAPTER 12

---

# BROKEN

*"If you're going through hell, keep going."*

Winston Churchill

Real life doesn't unfold like a movie or a TV show.

Writers and directors have time-tested devices at their disposal to increase tension, inform the audience, and let people know something of absolutely critical importance is about to take place.

*The music grows soft, then gradually builds in intensity until it abruptly stops.*

*The camera closes in on the faces of the main characters, panning across the room to reveal their response.*

*A phrase is repeated from an earlier foreshadowing in the story as a clue to the larger story taking place all along.*

In multimedia storytelling, these techniques prepare us for the emotional bomb about to detonate. Life doesn't afford us the same privilege.

Without much warning, with little preparation, life happens to us.

Sometimes this makes us feel like nothing significant is going on in our lives, and then all of sudden, we get knocked over.

It makes us feel helpless. It reminds us how small we are and how fragile life truly is.

These emotions and more collided on December 18, 2008, in my room at Baylor Grapevine Hospital.

♣ ♦ ♥ ♠

My family practitioner never would have made it as an actor.

I could tell he was trying his best to stay positive and encouraging, but I saw through his misdirection. It was the same approach I'd used hundreds of times to fool college students—he told me one thing but thought something completely different.

Over the past few weeks, I'd tried a series of different medications to manage the pain from what he'd described as blood clots in my leg. I knew blood clots moved, and if they went next to your heart, they could kill you. But I never expected them to hurt so much. My leg felt like it was exploding slowly from the inside out.

The physical pain was much more intense than anything I'd experienced, including the devastating shoulder injury that ended my baseball career.

Dr. Lee said that during the course of routine tests, they'd noticed my white blood cell count was "a bit high." I knew white blood cells were important—they helped fight off disease—if I remembered correctly. That didn't explain the excruciating pain.

It turned out my white blood cell count was slightly more than "a bit high"—*it was eight times higher than normal.*

With a calm demeanor, Dr. Lee assured me there were several non-serious explanations. They'd called in an oncologist to take a look at my charts to help figure out what was wrong. I didn't know what an oncologist was, but it sounded intelligent and professional, so I felt like everything was under control.

I had no idea an oncologist was a cancer specialist.

Before he left the room, Dr. Lee told me, *"You're going to be all right."*

A few moments later, my new oncologist, Dr. Drinkard, walked into my room, holding a clipboard. He was a heavy-set gentleman with salt-and-pepper hair, who looked serious and strong—the kind of guy who'd spent many days in life-and-death situations.

Slowly and carefully, he described what was happening in my body. The white blood cells were stuck in a loop. They made bad copies of bad cells at an accelerated rate, which crowded the bone marrow in my leg, causing it to swell like a balloon. My tibia was breaking from the inside out. As painful and dramatic as this was, there was a much greater problem.

Dr. Drinkard said, *"You have leukemia."*

What I heard was, *"You're going to die. Your wife will be alone, and your children will grow up without a father."*

Fear, panic, and anxiety swirled in my head. *What about a second opinion? Are we sure it's not a blood clot? How can this be happening?*

Dr. Drinkard wasn't finished.

*"You have a very aggressive form of leukemia called, 'Adult Acute Lymphoblastic Leukemia Lymphoma' (ALL). It's progressed to the stage where, without treatment, you'll be dead in two months because your kidneys will completely shut down."*

My condition was so serious, Dr. Drinkard had already scheduled a chest catheter procedure so we could begin chemotherapy immediately.

♣ ♦ ♥ ♠

It was like a bomb went off in our family.

We'd only begun to laugh and feel joy again following Tennyson's death—this was beyond too much, too soon.

The night I was diagnosed and admitted to the hospital, our three and a half-year-old daughter had her first dance recital. As I regretted missing her first performance, I wondered if I'd ever get the chance to see her dance.

She came to my hospital room still wearing her green Christmas tree outfit with matching frilly ribbon in her hair. The excitement of her performance hadn't worn off a bit.

She giggled as she repeated for me her favorite moments of the recital in a wonderful, one-girl encore. Our two-year-old son was undaunted by the tubes, machines, and poles surrounding me and hopped right up into bed.

For the first time since receiving my death sentence hours earlier, I found my resolve. I had too much to live for. I was going to fight.

Whatever it took, whatever the price, I was going to beat this.

♣ ♦ ♥ ♠

If I was going to defeat the leukemia, I needed a plan.

And at this point, there were more questions than answers.

- *How advanced was my condition?*
- *What would be the most effective form of treatment?*

- *Where would I go for treatment?*
- *How would all this impact Eli and the children?*

My father-in-law was a cancer survivor—he was also given a death sentence—stage four colon cancer. The doctors told him he had a few months to live, but he was determined to prove them wrong. He is an incredibly hard worker, has an iron will, and is a self-made man.

These traits were forged into his character, growing up on a cattle ranch in Northwestern Oklahoma, going on to become very successful in the oil and gas industry. He brought this same tough-as-nails attitude to his cancer fight and today celebrates more than a decade in complete remission.

He was as engaged and vocal as I'd ever seen him in all the time I'd known him. He wouldn't sit back and let his son-in-law die—more importantly, he had to do something for the father of his grandchildren … his little girl's husband.

This was a fight he knew how to win—and the greatest weapon he'd been given was the MD Anderson Cancer Center in Houston. He was adamant—that's where I'd go for treatment.

Its full name is The University of Texas MD Anderson Center, and it's widely regarded as the best cancer treatment facility in the world. In nine of the last eleven years (including 2012), *US News and World Report* recognized the facility as the best cancer hospital. Many of the most aggressive, cutting-edge techniques currently being developed are first implemented there. I had one chance to beat ALL, and there was no question MD Anderson gave me the best chance.

We quickly learned a patient cannot start treatment at one hospital then transfer to MD Anderson. If Dr. Drinkard even administered the chest catheter he'd already scheduled, I would be ineligible. When we told him our plan, he thought we were crazy: *How would I make it to Houston in my condition?*

Transportation wasn't the only issue—I had to be accepted into the program. Fortunately, my sister worked in the medical industry in San Jose, California, and had a connection with one of the top leukemia specialists.

While we waited to hear from MD Anderson, Dr. Drinkard continued to do tests to aid in the development of a treatment strategy once it became clear which hospital I'd be at long-term. He informed me he needed to do a bone marrow biopsy. Because I'd never seen the procedure performed, I imagined it was a lot like drawing blood.

Wrong.

He pulled out an instrument resembling an industrial-strength corkscrew and instructed me to lie on my stomach. Next, he climbed up and sat on my back. I'd been given a heavy hydromorphine drip when I was admitted, but I found out later, it's typical to be knocked out for this procedure. Once he drilled down into the bone of my hip, I prayed my body would knock itself out.

The pain was indescribable.

As he pulled out the sample of marrow, I saw it was unusually white ... an urgent sign of danger. The leukemia was very advanced and growing worse by the moment.

Leukemia comes from the Greek words for *"white"* and *"blood,"* and I'd now confirmed with my own eyes I was one of the more than 140,000 people in America diagnosed with the disease every year.

Every four minutes, someone in America finds out they have it, too. Leukemia accounts for nine percent of the new cancer cases discovered annually.

On December 23rd, two days before Christmas and five days after receiving a death sentence, my sister finally talked with her friend at MD Anderson. He told her he'd do everything he could to get me in. Later that night, medicated with the largest dose of the strongest painkillers I'd taken, I was loaded onto the private plane my father-in-law had arranged.

Two hours after exiting Baylor Grapevine in north Texas, I was wheeled into the 8th floor Leukemia Center at MD Anderson in Houston.

It would become my battleground, the site where leukemia and I would battle to the death. One of us was not going to make it. As I looked at the schedule waiting for me on the whiteboard at the foot of my bed, it was clear who was winning.

♣ ♦ ♥ ♠

ALL was thrashing my body. I underwent five grueling procedures before the end of the night.

The first procedure was the long-delayed chest catheter Dr. Drinkard wanted to do six days earlier. Imagine a large vein running along your chest. Now imagine an incision in your chest large enough for a rubber tube with two hanging pieces of plastic where intense chemo treatments could be pumped quickly through your blood.

Next, I was given a spinal tap to examine whether or not the leukemia had spread into my spine. Essentially, the doctor/technician inserted a drumstick-size needle into my spine. This made my body tingle and jerk in very specific spots from my head to my toes. I couldn't sleep or be knocked out because during the procedure, I had to tell them how each prick with the needle in my spine made me feel.

Thankfully, the spinal tap came back with a clean report, but there was no time to celebrate. I was headed to the CAT Scan—the claustrophobia-inducing tube straight out of a 1960s sci-fi movie that they stick patients in. It was creepy, but it wasn't painful, but the bone marrow biopsy I had done before getting to MD Anderson made up for that.

The thought of the barbaric, torture-like corkscrew device still makes my toes curl.

Finally, after lying highly-sedated in a hospital bed for six days, I'd developed a few issues with my "internal plumbing." They gave me a serum to clean me out, but it was so explosively efficient, "treat hemorrhoids" was added as an unexpected, bonus sixth procedure.

From 2007-2008, I'd suffered some incredibly difficult days. This may have been the worst. I wasn't simply exhausted. I was more than sick with a terminal disease.

Finally, I was broken.

Alone on Christmas Eve in a tiny, cramped hospital room with tubes sticking out of my chest, a pee jar hanging on a rack, and a crude make-shift toilet on the floor, I snapped.

Anger, frustration, and a deep sense of betrayal filled my thoughts, and this time there was no holding them back. Circulating, they grew in strength and intensity.

*Thanks, God. This is a nice touch. Instead of celebrating 'Your birth' with my family, I'm dying alone in a hospital bed.*

*It wasn't enough for You to do nothing while my brother, my partner in ministry, died. You decided to come back and finish the job. You're going to get rid of me, too. WHERE ARE YOU? What about all those promises You made?*

I'd never been so angry. I don't know if I had ever felt any emotion more intensely.

*Forget You. No ... SCREW You! Go ahead, kill me. I'm not serving You anymore. What kind of God are You? You take away my baseball career, the ministry tries to keep me from marrying Eli, Tennyson dies, and now this?*

To this point, the conversation existed purely in my thoughts. Thoughts I believed with my whole being, but they were internal. Unspoken.

But the rage, the pain, and the disappointment culminated in two words that wouldn't stay silent. Two words I never thought I'd speak again.

They jumped out of me, pointed like a laser at God.

*"F*** You."*

# CHAPTER 13

---

# THE CAPE

*"We have two options medically and emotionally:*
*Give up or fight like hell."*

Lance Armstrong

Merry Christmas.

It's supposed to be the best day of the year ... but not in 2008. Not only was it the worst day of the year for me—it was the worst day of my life.

My children were in Santa Fe, New Mexico, trying their best to celebrate and keep some sense of normalcy. For a child, Christmas is the greatest day of the year—lots of sugar, stockings, and a mountain of presents. Even if I couldn't be there with them, I wanted them to celebrate with their grandparents instead of worrying about their father.

At least, I thought I wanted them to. I told Eli and her parents it was fine, and at the time, it seemed like the noble, courageous decision any good father would make.

Now I wasn't so sure. While they were eating a beautiful breakfast, drinking cocoa by the tree and opening presents, their mom and dad were stuck in a tiny hospital room, fighting for the future of our family. Every two hours, nurses came in and took my blood.

My only Christmas gift didn't need to be opened; it needed to be signed—the paperwork necessary to start my chemotherapy.

It all seemed like a cruel, sick joke.

And at that particular moment, not only did I believe God was ignoring my prayers, I believed He was the one toying with my life.

♣ ♦ ♥ ♠

The world's greatest expert on *Adult Acute Lymphoblastic Leukemia (ALL)*, Dr. Debbie Thomas, works at MD Anderson. Receiving treatment and care from Dr. Thomas was one of the reasons we took such drastic steps to move me down to Houston.

Cancer is an insidious disease. Not only does it attack your body by violently pitting your own cells against each other at a molecular level, it also attacks your mind and your emotions. The aching, exhausting, relentless physical pain is bad enough ... but it's only one of cancer's weapons. No matter where in your body it's located, cancer wages war on your mind psychologically and on your heart by tearing away your emotions layer by layer.

You can't make friends with it. You can't learn to live with it. Cancer doesn't play nice, it's not fair, and it won't make deals with you.

It's a stone cold killer.

If you're going to survive, you have to declare all-out war. You have to confront the brutal facts every morning with relentless tenacity because that's exactly how your enemy comes at you.

Lance Armstrong is one of the most famous cancer survivors in the world—after his cancer went into remission, he went on to win the Tour de France seven years in a row. I realize there's speculation swirling around his career regarding the use of performance-enhancing methods. I have no idea if he cheated, but I do know he never stopped fighting. His foundation has donated millions to MD Anderson, and they made those little yellow "Live Strong" bracelets cool enough for non-cancer patients to wear them.

The patients at MD Anderson needed something more intense than those famous little yellow bracelets. They were facing the most drastic, lethal forms of cancer, and they needed a message with a greater sense of urgency. Their bracelets were black, and in huge letters, they simply read, *"F*** Cancer."*

I loved those bracelets.

If I was going to make it through this, I realized I had to get a chip on my shoulder. I had to break down all my self-pity, my discouragement, my depression, my fear and channel it all into fight and determination.

And while I broke down my negative emotions, the chemo started to break down my sick, decaying body.

♣ ♦ ♥ ♠

The science behind chemotherapy treatments goes back to the use of mustard gas as a chemical weapon in World War I and a variation used in World War II. Every form of cancer involves some form of uncontrollable cell growth; the chemotherapy cycle is designed to slow and eventually stop this process.

Because my white blood cells were the ones growing out of control, killing them meant tearing down my immune system in order to rebuild it.

I had to wear a mask and take every precaution to constantly sanitize my environments. Not only was this uncomfortable and difficult, it was emotionally devastating. It meant I couldn't see my children because of my inability to fight off germs.

My chemo treatment was scheduled on a 21-day cycle, and the first round, most commonly referred to as "Hyper CVAD," required four full days of hospitalization. The very first chemical they brought into drip through my chest catheter was a massive bright yellow bag. The sensation of these drugs entering my chest is difficult to describe—I felt the cool, liquid solution dripping, and in a few moments, I felt a burning sensation.

What makes it so miserable are all the little things. I couldn't take a shower because of the risk of infection. I had to wheel the racks with the hanging bags wherever I went. I watched TV for only so long before I began to hate it.

The hardest part was mental. I was stuck in a tiny room, trying to think about anything other than the cold reality that a murderous disease that kills millions around the world every year had turned its gaze on me.

After the first four days, I was moved to a temporary housing facility connected to MD Anderson. The idea behind this "hotel" is kind and well-intentioned—give patients and their loved ones affordable housing so they can love and support cancer victims fighting for their lives—but the reality is far more depressing.

Every day, new families came in—sad, tear-stained faces, agonizing over the family member who'd recently received a death sentence.

Once I adjusted to the constant presence of tubes, rolling carts, catheters, and the unusual sensation that accompanied the process of the bags dripping directly into my chest, I actually felt pretty good.

I didn't tell anyone, but I quietly thought to myself, *This chemo thing really isn't too bad.* I didn't realize the side-effects don't show up until day six.

You know how your skin on the inside of your mouth feels after taking a big bite of scalding hot soup? The pain from the burn stings, the flesh loses feeling before peeling over the next 24 hours or so, and then you taste your own blood and seared flesh throughout the sensitive area.

On the sixth morning, I woke to this terrible feeling ... in my entire body ... like being fried from the inside out.

The chemo doesn't target only the patient's white blood cells; it seeks and destroys all the fast-growing cells in his body. This causes his hair to fall out and his finger nails to stop growing.

There's no way to explain this feeling to someone who's never experienced it. I reached my fingers into my hair to scratch an itch on my scalp, and when I pulled it back, huge clumps of hair came with it. It didn't hurt ... the hairs slipped right out of their follicles.

Day six kicked my ass. I lacked the strength to get out of bed, the pain was crippling, and I struggled to even sit up. But I couldn't rest. I had to go back to the hospital for blood work, blood clot shots, Neupogen shots (to accelerate the growth of the new, healthy white blood cells), and, if needed, a blood transfusion.

Even when I wasn't admitted to the hospital, I was there for testing from five to ten hours a day. I repeated this cycle, EVERY DAY, from day six until day 21. The whole thing is insane—intentionally destroying your immune system, hoping you might be able to rebuild it. There are no guarantees.

The process emaciates you to the point you barely look human. You're so frail and fragile you couldn't possibly survive in the outside world, and you must stock up on the surprisingly above-average food at MD Anderson just to find the strength to go from one test to the next.

Months before my diagnosis, I recorded a live interview with James Robison for his television show *Life Today*. The episode aired during one of my hospital stays. While I watched myself on a small hospital TV, a nurse walked in to draw my blood. I pointed to myself on TV and asked if she recognized "that guy." She, of course, didn't recognize me. I didn't blame her. My baldhead and gaunt look would have fooled anybody. I told her the guest on the show was me. She looked at me strangely, thought me delusional, and did not believe me. I think she thought I was crazy. It was humbling, to say the least.

I wasn't ready for day six the first time I experienced it, but once my treatment cycle came to an end, I discovered it wasn't the worst day. The real low moment was day 21. By that point in the process, my body was just starting to feel better. Right when I regained the ability to taste my food and enjoy a good meal, the whole cycle resets.

And this time I knew exactly what was coming.

♣ ♦ ♥ ♠

I never wore the black bracelet. I had something better.

Our son, Gavin, loved Superman, and he showed the world his deep-seated love for the Man of Steel by wearing his Superman cape wherever he went. Clark Kent never wore the cape as often as Gavin did—at the grocery store, the mall, both fast-food and traditional restaurants, even at church.

When he wore the cape, he felt invincible and faster than a speeding bullet. After my first round of chemo, Eli came to see me, but she didn't come alone.

Gavin sent his cape because his daddy needed it.

Fighting back the tears, I wrapped that cape around my fist like a boxing glove and squeezed as hard as I could. The cape didn't leave my hand.

My goal changed that day. In one moment, it all became so clear. I wasn't simply going to beat cancer. I was going to be there for my family. I refused to let cancer steal my son's little league games, my daughter's dance recitals, or any of the graduations, colleges, weddings, and grandkids waiting for us down the road.

Eli wasn't going to be a widow. No matter what, Daddy was coming home. I didn't care if it took 50, 100, or 200 cycles of chemo. I was ready.

Unfortunately, even if I endured 1000 treatments, it wouldn't have mattered. Chemo couldn't fix my problem.

♣ ♦ ♥ ♠

Doctors and researchers are able to test and study the chromosomal details of leukemia. This microscopic level of detail revealed a serious problem.

My initial diagnosis was wrong.

I didn't have *ALL*. I had an extremely rare and devastating form of the disease known as *Philadelphia Positive Acute Lymphoblastic Lymphoma* (PH+ ALL). Because of the abnormalities this condition causes at the genetic level, even if the chemotherapy kills the cancer, it won't stay dead. The cancer will continue to come back.

If I was going to beat PH+ ALL, I had only one option left, and it was a long shot. And because of my weakened condition and the aggressive nature of my disease, I was a poor candidate.

My only chance, my last hope, was a bone marrow transplant.

# CHAPTER 14

---

# 1 IN 9 MILLION

> Valerie: **"Think it'll work?"**
> Miracle Max: **"It would take a miracle."**
> Carol Kane and Billy Crystal, *The Princess Bride*

Tennyson and I re-branded our performance around the word *"maze"* because it was filled with intrigue, mystery, dead ends, and the constant invitation to pursue answers.

We had no idea how poignantly our decision would forecast not only the next couple of years, but as it turned out, the end of our lives. Our intention was to use MAZE to describe the experience our audience would undergo, not to predict our own demise.

Etymologists believe the word *"maze"* was first used around the year 1300 A.D. from Old English roots meaning *"to confuse"* or *"to confound."* Another word for *"maze"* is *"labyrinth,"* made famous by the Greek myth that tells the story about a magician/inventor who built the massive structure to imprison the Minotaur.

I never saw a freakish half-man/half-bull, axe-wielding monster, but I was certain someone (or something) was trying to kill me. It was the same sensation I'd felt the night I'd miraculously walked away from the deadly crash in my truck in the earliest days of our magic career.

There was no way all the chaos, confusion, conflict, and tragedy that had become my life was arbitrary. I couldn't shake the feeling that from a different perspective, the string of horrific events over the past several years were related. There were answers to the mystery—someone had built this maze, and was watching me struggle through it.

At certain points, I attributed our opposition to dark powers—evil, demonic spirits determined to intimidate, attack, and discourage us from using magic to tell people about a God Who loved them and cared deeply about their daily lives.

But as the soul-crushing challenges kept coming over and over, my perspective changed. Now my issue was with God. I was convinced the One Who created the heavens and the earth, also created the maze I'd been living in—which had become my own personal hell.

When Tennyson died, I gave up—it was like life just stopped. I sat down in the maze and refused to move. Slowly, over time, I got back up, did some shows, found a new partner, and started making my way through the labyrinth.

And then I was diagnosed with *Adult Acute Lymphoblastic Leukemia*, and the bottom dropped out. All the progress I'd made was gone in an instant. My legs were literally cut out from under me.

I thought the most tragic event of my life was in my past. But before my 30th birthday, a little more than a year after watching my brother die, I was told I had months to live. And yet because of the loving support of my family, I didn't lie down in the maze and quit. I wanted to give up, but I didn't.

Somehow, I kept going.

With the expertise and aid of MD Anderson, I started to believe I could make my way out. The chemo was way worse than I'd feared, but, at least, I was moving forward. However microscopic it may have been, there was a chance I'd get through this.

But the chemo ended up being one more dead end. No matter how many times we fried the cancer from my insides out, it would keep growing back. Either the chemo treatments or my hyper-aggressive white blood cells were going to kill me. My diagnosis had been wrong—I was part of the small minority of leukemia cases known as PH+ALL.

There was only one way out of the maze. I needed a new immune system. I had a few months to find a perfect bone marrow match.

♣ ♦ ♥ ♠

After two rounds of chemotherapy, I was no longer a cancer patient—not because I'd beaten the disease ... because my current treatment plan could NEVER beat it.

I was now officially a transplant patient. More tests, new doctors, and back on a waiting list.

My new doctor explained exactly what I was up against:

- If my body responded to the chemo treatments ...
- If my cancer went into remission ...

- If we found a bone marrow donor ...
- And if my body was strong enough to be a viable recipient ...

I would be eligible for a revolutionary surgical procedure where, on average, two out of every three patients survive.

The last thing my new doctor said to me was, *"It's time to put on your boxing gloves."*

I understood what he was trying to prepare me for, but he didn't understand I'd been fighting for my life every day for the last few years. My metaphorical boxing gloves had been on so long, I'd forgotten what life was like outside the ring.

Some fights I'd won—Eli and I overcame serious adversity and managed to save our marriage. After I thought the dream had died, somehow we'd been able to resurrect MAZE magic.

But every single day, I mourned the losses. When my best friend and brother needed me most, I wasn't there, and I'd lost the will to fight off my doubts, my skepticism, and my deep sense of betrayal. My relationship with Jesus was shattered and broken—perhaps beyond repair.

All my energy and focus had been directed toward chemotherapy—I gripped Gavin's cape in my fist, prepared myself for the two 21-day cycles, and gritted my teeth. And now, chemo was only the beginning of a much longer, much more grueling journey.

Every fighter studies his opponent to discover exactly what he's up against. I went online to do a little research. I needed to know what my chances were.

Google sent me to a series of websites, ranging from the clinics and research facilities to personal stories of survivors. The survival rate for PH+ALL bone marrow transplant recipients was roughly 20 percent.

In other words, in a group of five patients, only one would cheat death.

♣ ♦ ♥ ♠

While I returned for another round of chemo, the donor search began with my younger sister, Hayley. She had helped get us into MD Anderson (a huge contribution), but she wanted to do more. She was the most likely candidate, and she desperately wanted to be a match and give me the bone marrow I needed to rebuild my immune system.

It was a moment of hope. My doctors at MD Anderson were encouraged by the impact the chemo was having on my system. The cancer was retreating into remission—it was only a matter of time before it returned, but it wasn't getting worse.

We had a window to find a match.

Finding a match has nothing to do with blood type. Five different pairs of proteins on a small section of chromosomes on the surface of the white blood cells are examined and cross-referenced to find a match. At least six of the ten must line up in order to continue pursuing the possibility of a transplant. The chances of finding a perfect match (10 out of 10) outside of a sibling are approximately 1 in 100,000.

70 percent of leukemia patients don't have a match in their family, and so they rely on the National Marrow Donor Program (NMDP), also known as the "Be the Match Foundation."

Hayley would have walked from California to give me her bone marrow and save my life, but when her test results came back, we learned I was part of the 70 percent. We were devastated.

If I was going to find a match, it would be a total stranger who had decided to donate his or her bone marrow without knowing it would determine whether or not Eli would be a widow or my children would grow up without their father.

We shipped my information off to the NMDP in Minneapolis, Minnesota, and waited for more test results.

The obvious question, *"What are the odds of finding a match?"* is met with a nearly identical response throughout the medical community:

*"Well ... it depends. Some people have hundreds of potential matches. Other people have none. Until we run your results, we won't know."*

No one likes to wait. But this isn't the ordinary, inconvenient form of waiting, like wondering when your package from Amazon will show up at your door.

This is waiting for a pardon while you're sitting on death row, counting down the days before your execution.

I wasn't in a jail cell. I spent between four to eight hours, sometimes more, every day, shuffling back and forth between my apartment, the doctor's office, and the hospital, going through more rounds of aggressive chemo.

Another month passed, another round of chemo, and no word from the NMDP. After another month and another round of chemo, we finally heard back from Minneapolis.

It wasn't the news we were hoping for. Out of the more than 9 million donors registered at the NMDP, 16 were potential matches.

Not 16,000. Not 1600. 16.

**CHANCES OF DYING IN A CAR CRASH DURING YOUR LIFETIME:**

1 IN 100

**CHANCES OF BEING STRUCK BY LIGHTNING IN YOUR LIFETIME:**

1 IN 100,000

**CHANCES OF BEING ATTACKED BY A SHARK IN YOUR LIFETIME:**

1 IN 11.5 MILLION

**CHANCES OF WINNING THE POWERBALL LOTTERY:**

1 IN 175 MILLION

There was more. The key word in the sentence was *"potential"*—my *"Sweet 16"* had to be tested further to determine how many weren't merely promising but were actually a viable match.

Even a perfect match wasn't a guarantee. The donor had to undergo a complete physical to determine whether he or she was healthy enough to endure the rigors of the harvesting process.

As bad as the odds seemed, Eli and I clung to hope. Out of 16 potentials, we needed only one.

I was dying from tainted, poisoned blood killing me from the inside out. I needed a substitute, an advocate. I needed a single donor who could be my perfect match.

Then it dawned on me like a giant, neon sign, guiding my way through the terrifying maze. I wasn't being hunted. I was being pursued. The designer of the maze wasn't trying to torment me, but point me to a greater truth.

I literally needed the exact solution I'd spent the past five years communicating to young people. I needed to open my eyes to the deeper reality around me. If I could look past my confusion and my pain, if I could set aside my doubts and my anger, I would discover my only hope was in the same place it had always been.

What I needed was a savior—someone with perfect, uncontaminated blood who would be willing to shed his or her blood to give me new life.

And then it happened. The call came. On my way back for another round of chemo, the NMDP called. I put the call on speaker so Eli and I could hear it together.

*"I have some good news for you. Out of the 16 potential matches, there was one perfect match. A ten out of ten."* The staff had contacted the donor who agreed to move forward with the transplant.

*"Due to our confidentiality agreement, the only thing we can tell you about this person is your match is a 19-year-old-female."*

Not only did my donor embody the message I'd communicated to crowds of students in more cities and on more campuses than I could remember, she looked like them. She was *them*.

The one in nine million I needed turned out to be the primary demographic of MAZE's audience. Eli, my children, Tennyson, and I had all paid a great price to make a difference in the lives of 19 year-old-girls.

Now one I'd never met had come forward to save mine.

♣ ♦ ♥ ♠

Great stories are filled with mystery, intrigue, conflict, and twists all leading up to a beautifully subtle moment of enlightenment. It doesn't hit you over the head ... it slowly dawns on you. In time, the shadows disappear, and in their place, you discover awe and wonder.

*You realize Bruce Willis has been dead all along. (Sixth Sense)*

*You discover Keyser Soze has been sitting in the police station the entire time. (The Usual Suspects)*

*You recognize it wasn't about building a baseball stadium in a cornfield or meeting the ghost of Shoeless Joe—it was always about Ray having a catch with his dad. (Field of Dreams)*

It's easier to watch a great story than to live one.

When you're the main character, there's nowhere to hide from the pain, the tragedy, and the necessary narrative arc. You experience the fullness of it all in real time. Only in hindsight can you appreciate the artistry—and you always need help to see what's been there the whole time.

Although I'd doubted Him, blamed Him for every problem, turned my back on Him, and cursed His name, God never left me. I didn't have to know what He was up to in order to give Him permission to keep His hand on my life.

We weren't out of the woods yet. I still had all kinds of issues, questions, and hurts, but for the first time in a long time, I could see what He was up to.

# CHAPTER 15

---

# THE HEALING POWER OF DEATH

*"Every man dies. Not every man really lives."*

Mel Gibson as William Wallace, *Braveheart*

Cancer was no longer my issue.

In the eyes of the hospital, I wasn't even a cancer patient. Long days spent in the hospital would now take place in a whole new area of MD Anderson. My future, my only hope, my game plan was now described with one word: *transplant*.

I wasn't a cancer survivor. I hadn't survived anything yet. Yes, I was very blessed to find a potential transplant donor, like one in nine million blessed, but I had a long way to go. It was dense, dark forest as far as I could see with all kinds of spooky noises and predators lying in wait for me.

My new doctor, Dr. Giralt, was straight out of central casting with a New York accent so strong, you'd expect to see him in a Woody Allen film or as a memorable, supporting character on *Seinfeld*. Without the white jacket with the shirt and tie, you would've bet your paycheck he was the patient, not the doctor.

And now my life was in his hands.

*"Mis-tah Muun-Rooow,"* he would say—and I learned what followed would be cold, hard truth.

He had the bedside manner of a drill sergeant; no fluff, no false hope. If he read Jim Collins' classic book *Good to Great,* the part he remembered was *"Confront the brutal facts."*

That's precisely what we did every time we met. It was difficult, but I learned to appreciate it. It was exactly what I needed.

When going into a war, you don't want a kindergarten teacher with you—you want a grizzled, battle-tested sergeant. You want Colonel Nathan Jessup (Jack Nicholson, *A Few Good Men*) because you want him on that wall. You need him on that wall.

This was the situation as Dr. Giralt described it for me: my procedure was a toss-up. 50/50. It could go either way. He knew I'd played baseball, so he gave me a simple, relatable metaphor.

The doctors were going to put the ball on the tee, and then my job was to hit the ball out the park.

*What?!?*

I thought the impossible, life-and-death challenge was finding the donor, not living through the transplant.

Wrong.

It turned out the transplant process was more grueling, more painful, more taxing than chemotherapy.

Batter up.

♣ ♦ ♥ ♠

My transplant team told me to focus all my strength and determination toward *"The 100 Days."*

The number refers to the average time a successful transplant takes—from the moment the patient checks into the hospital for the procedure to the time he's considered well enough to leave and begin the next phase of recovery.

My transplant was scheduled for three days after my April 23rd birthday, which meant, my 100 days would last until August 3rd. If I survived the first 30 days, every one of them would be spent on the 10th floor of MD Anderson. In order to receive a new immune system, my old one had to be completely destroyed, and when you have no immune system, even the smallest, most insignificant microbe can be deadly.

In some strange, bizarre way, it sounded like a David Blaine illusion in an over-the-top, made-for-TV special. But it wasn't an illusion, and it wasn't a TV show. It was my life ... my future ... my family's and loved ones' last hope.

But before I got to day 30, I'd have to survive the first 10—10 days of the most aggressive, intense chemotherapy I'd endured yet with the sole goal of killing the immune system I was born with. It was killing me ... so one of us had to die if I had any real chance to live.

♣ ♦ ♥ ♠

When you're a kid, turning 30 seems crazy. Thirty makes you an old man. But once you finish college, 30 looks a lot different. It's on the front end of adulthood, not the middle, and certainly not the end.

For my 30th birthday, Eli and I celebrated while I gritted my way through the seventh day of the most taxing chemotherapy I'd ever known. Eli was amazing. She transformed my drab hospital room into a cheesy-beach wonderland. It was gloriously tacky, and she even brought me a goofy, paper crown.

April 23rd was approaching. The drugs were so strong, I could eat only a small serving of Cream of Wheat in the morning, and yet the impact of the chemo drugs caused enough bloating and water retention for me to gain 50 pounds in only a few days.

One more bizarre side-effect of this ridiculous sci-fi process ...

By the time I left the hospital in 30 days, I'd lose those 50 pounds, plus 50 more. Huge swings in my weight weren't the only side-effects. I had strange, powerfully lucid hallucinations on a regular basis. There was not much to do stuck in bed all day beyond watching TV, but my ability to pay attention was so weakened, I couldn't follow even the most basic, formulaic TV shows.

Yet none of this mattered. Everything rested on Day 10. That's when we flipped the coin. The 50/50 would be resolved. In the course of an hour, my body would accept the new bone marrow, and I'd take one giant step toward recovery, or it would reject it, and I would die.

♣ ♦ ♥ ♠

Blood is liquid life. It carries oxygen and nutrients to your cells while removing waste. I'd read in the Bible, *"The life of every creature is in its blood."* Leviticus 17:14 NLT, but now, I understood what it meant on an extremely personal level.

A patient with healthy blood and failing internal organs can continue to live on because of this life-giving power of blood, but once the blood was poisoned or tainted, it had to be replaced. A sacrifice had to be made. New blood needed to flow through my veins if I wanted to continue living.

Day 10 had finally arrived. Dr. Giralt told me April 23rd would become my "new birthday." It could've been any day, and yet, it came three days after my actual birthday. Even through the grogginess of the medication, I seemed to remember Someone else Who died and rose again three days later.

I would be a totally new person because someone else would be living on the inside of me through the blood she sacrificed so I could live.

If I wanted to truly live, the "old me" had to die.

In order to save my life, I had to lose it.

Could it be any clearer?

Apparently, God thought I was slow, a little too dense to pick up on subtle nuances, so He delivered a message so unmistakable, so closely resembling the process of salvation, I wouldn't have missed it had I been asleep.

It's hard to believe my Jewish, agnostic doctor never stopped and recognized how his detailed descriptions of what was about to take place related to the most fundamental tenant of historic Christianity. He even said, *"You're going to be born again. It's as if you're going to be a baby inside the womb, all over again."*

The irony of my faith in the Gospel being restored through my unbelieving doctor was not lost on me. Every time he said a phrase like this to me, I was filled with the same sense of awe and wonder that made me fall in love with both magic—and God—in the first place.

It didn't take away the pain and the sadness I'd experienced over the past couple of years, but the mystery and the wonder were slowly returning to my life.

My faith and my soul were being healed, but there was still a long way to go in the recovery of my body. I realized again the fragile and unpredictable nature of my condition and the precariousness of my pending procedure after signing my signature more than 70 times on all kinds of release forms.

Apparently MD Anderson was concerned I would die and my family would sue. Not exactly the most comforting thought pre-surgery.

Before the procedure on April 23rd, I was allowed to go to a Mexican restaurant in the Museum District with Eli, the kids, and my in-laws to celebrate my birthday. I couldn't escape the thought that this might be the last time I would see them. I was torn between saying nothing and saying goodbye. On one hand, I needed to stay positive and hopeful, but, on the other hand, I didn't want my children unprepared if this was the last time we were together.

After dinner, Eli drove me to the hospital with a bag packed to get me through those first 30 days. We had no guarantee I would live to use all of them, but we hoped and prayed every one of those shirts, pants, and boxers would be washed again.

I was so scared. And helpless.

I cried that night and asked God to help. I was trusting Him to heal me, but if He didn't, I wanted Him to care for my young family.

When you realize you're going to die, to be given a chance to live again changes everything. Each day, each moment, each laugh shared with a loved one or a drink of water or a beautiful sunset becomes a gift.

So many people wander through life, bored, disengaged, and unappreciative. They might have a pulse, but they're not really alive.

But once you've been dead, there's no such thing as an ordinary day. They're all spectacular.

♣ ♦ ♥ ♠

They brought the bag of new blood to my room, and everyone cleared out. I was too drugged to realize it, but the nurses pulled Eli out before they turned on the drip.

During those 60 minutes, a nurse stayed by my side and monitored even the slightest fluctuation in pulmonary activity. This was the coin-flip: either my body would accept the new blood, giving me a chance to finally beat the cancer, or it would reject the new blood, and I would die.

The new, life-saving blood started dripping into my system around 2 p.m.—and for the next hour, Eli endured the most stressful, gut-wrenching, nail-biting moments of her life.

The world doesn't usually work this way: *"Wait here for an hour. Find a magazine. Grab a cup of coffee. Hang out. When we come get you, we'll tell you whether or not you're going to be a widow."*

The staff at MD Anderson is world-class, and they certainly didn't say anything close to this, but they may as well have.

That's how it felt for Eli. It may have been harder on her than it was on me. Sixty minutes feels like an eternity when you're waiting to find out if your husband will live or die.

The nurses had a nickname for the primary drug used in this procedure: *"Shake and bake."* Once the medicine took affect, it was common for the patient's temperature to rise as high as 105 degrees for an extended period of time—that was *"the bake."* The other noticeable side-effect was aggressive twitching and convulsions in the teeth, shoulders, and legs—*"the shake."*

When the staff finally came back to Eli, she sobbed. But it was good news. It was working.

For the moment, my body had accepted the new blood.

# CHAPTER 16

---

# BE THE MATCH

*"Only half of all patients who would benefit from a life-saving marrow transplant actually receive one."*

Christine Flemming, President, Be the Match Foundation

Teenage girls rule the world.

Hundreds of millions of dollars of advertising campaigns beg for their attention every year because when they love something, they have the discretionary income to prove their love.

And when they prove their love, money is no object. They'll relentlessly beg Mom and Dad for what they want until their parents finally give in. They send hundreds of text messages every day. They wait in line for hours. They scream. They cry.

They're an unstoppable and combustible combination of stubborn will and raging hormones, and they have the power to transform relative unknowns into worldwide icons.

Without teenage girls, the world never enjoys the Beatles.

Without teenage girls, Michael Jackson never becomes the King of Pop.

Without teenage girls, Justin Bieber is just a goofy kid with a dorky haircut.

Without teenage girls, there's no Team Jacob, no Team Edward, and no awful, angst-ridden vampire-werewolf-Kristen Stewart love triangles.

And without one teenage girl—I would be dead, Eli would be a widow, and my children would be fatherless.

♣ ♦ ♥ ♠

When the doctors look at my blood, they see XX chromosomes, which means unlike most guys, I literally can get in touch with my feminine side.

All I have to do is prick my finger. I bleed lady blood.

I'd survived the transplant, and my body was adjusting, but I could barely look at myself in the mirror. I had no hair on my body at all. Being bald has become much more common, but there's still something really unsettling about a guy with no eyebrows ... so creepy and off-putting. It didn't help I was 60 pounds below my typical weight, my ribs were poking out, and my face was swollen from the steroids.

I spent most days stuck in bed, watching movies and entire seasons of TV shows, but my mind struggled to follow plot twists. This would frustrate anyone, but for a magician like me who'd spent hundreds of hours developing the ability to watch closely and notice what everyone else missed, it was infuriating.

It was like going crazy in slow motion.

Despite all these challenges, my recovery was progressing according to our plan. After 30 days, I moved out of MD Anderson into a nearby apartment. It wasn't a huge change though, since I still spent as many as 12 hours daily at the facility, going home only to sleep. On some visits, I was scheduled for blood transfusions, but blood is distributed on a first-come-first-serve basis, so there were days when we'd wait all day and go home empty.

The apartment had one incredible feature—the kids could stay with us. Seeing their beautiful, brave, loving faces was exactly what I needed. Each day I got to see, hear, laugh, and play with the reasons I had to beat this thing.

Once you've spent time on your deathbed, wondering if you'd ever see them again, you'll never hug your children the same way. You squeeze tighter, you kiss them more often, you smell the top of their heads longer, you linger when you hold their soft, little hands, and you learn to appreciate every second.

As baffling as it may sound, this was one of the greatest gifts PH+ ALL gave me—there are no ordinary, boring, mundane days for me. Everything we experience as a family is a gift.

Before long, *"The 100 Days"* were finished, and on August 2, 2009, I moved back home to be with my family.

I still bathed regularly in hand sanitizer, feared exposure to germs in public places like restaurants or the grocery store, and could be on my feet only a few hours before I needed to lie down and rest. I had good days where I felt myself adjusting and getting stronger and days when I couldn't keep down even the smallest snack.

My new doctor in Dallas communicated with MD Anderson and provided fantastic ongoing care. I was improving each day, so we began to talk about what my new normal would look like. My doctor asked me what I did for a living. When I told him about MAZE, his expression immediately confirmed what I'd feared.

Frequent travel and interacting with large crowds would test the limits of anyone's immune system, but for me, it could be disastrous.

He suggested it was time to start thinking about a new line of work.

Clearly there was wisdom in this perspective, but I couldn't shake the feeling giving up on MAZE would be letting Tennyson down. I wrestled with the idea. On one hand, so much had happened over the past few years. T wouldn't simply have been supportive—he would've made me promise to take care of myself so I could be there for my family. He loved Eli and the kids like his own family.

Not "like"—we *were* family.

My decision and the future of MAZE could wait. When I first went into treatment, we promised the kids when I was done, we'd take a family trip to Disneyland to celebrate.

On a beautiful, sunny November day in 2009, Disneyland truly was the Magic Kingdom, the happiest place on Earth. My little girl got a Cinderella dress complete with a tiara and sparkly shoes. We held hands as we walked down Main Street, soaking it all in.

I was still deep in the process of recovering, and I was exhausted most of the day ... but it was *perfect*.

Coming back to the place where so many of my own favorite childhood memories had taken place led me to reflect on everything that had happened in my life. I had experienced enough emotion and drama for multiple lifetimes; baseball dreams realized then lost, dreams of performing magic shows fulfilled then threatened by the power of death.

Yet, as a father, there's nothing like seeing your children laughing, smiling, and overflowing with joy. There's no way for me to communicate how fulfilling it is.

The memory of that glorious day will stay with me forever—if I close my eyes, I can return there instantly in my mind.

I feel the breeze against my cheeks. I smell the fresh baked churros. I hear the laughter of my children, running ahead to the next ride. I see a smile on Eli's face—bright enough to light up *It's a Small World*—with no trace of the anxiety and stress that had been her constant companions the past few years.

I wasn't the only one getting better—our entire family experienced a significant healing that day.

♣ ♦ ♥ ♠

Something changed while we were in Southern California. Going back to where it all began brought new clarity and confidence. I didn't need to pray about MAZE any more, consult any doctors, or wonder what was next. I knew.

I was ready to start doing shows again.

When I told my board of directors, they thought I was crazy. I don't blame them—I looked like a hot mess. The first sprouts of my recently returned hair looked more like chicken feathers than anything resembling a normal haircut.

Donald Trump thought it looked weird.

Strangely enough, this wasn't even my most unusual feature. Another side-effect of the healing process was a series of disgustingly large boils of puss on my feet and toes. Shoes and socks only agitated them, so I wore sandals everywhere … all through winter. I was quite a site.

In January 2010, MAZE made its triumphant return at Southern Methodist University in Dallas. My show had been radically transformed—I didn't need to talk philosophy and worldview to capture hearts and attention between illusions.

My story … what God had done in my life … was more than enough. Everything was so fresh and still settling in my mind, it felt like I was beginning to understand all the intricacies each time I told it. Some new detail, some unmistakable sign of God's providence, would become clear to me with every telling.

I had to carefully pace myself, but being with people and watching the way my story impacted them was a huge benefit to my healing process. Talking about it filled me with awe and wonder and an undeniable sense of gratitude.

The audience responded to the new show, too.

My body was still adjusting. I had no idea what "shingles" were. I thought they were those little strips you put on roofs, but apparently, they're also an extremely painful skin condition.

Shingles are unpleasant and irritating, but they're no big deal to a guy who's been raised from the dead—physically and spiritually.

I performed two of the biggest shows I'd ever done, shingles and all, at the University of Southern Illinois Edwardsville. More than 1200 students packed into the auditorium, and I was told another 2000 were turned away because of the fire code.

There was a new emotional energy, an undeniable relational connection between the audience and me in the new show. I began to realize how pain, adversity, and tragedy create an opportunity to connect with others in a powerful way. The mysteries in our own lives make more sense when we hear about the wonder and awe in someone else's.

But there was one piece of my puzzle I couldn't stop thinking about: *the mysterious teenage girl.* Who was this incredible stranger? Why did she do it? How in the world could I ever possibly thank her for what she'd done?

I had to meet her. I needed to see my one in nine million long shot … my perfect match.

♣ ♦ ♥ ♠

As a matter of policy, the NMDP keeps the records of all marrow donors completely sealed for the first year. It makes sense. They don't want recipients or their families chasing down donors.

On April 23, 2010, exactly one year to the day after I received my marrow transplant, I called MD Anderson and requested the contact information for the young woman who forever changed my family's life. My hands shook with nervous excitement as I waited to learn the identity of my mysterious teenage savior, but the administrative staff at MD Anderson told me the donor had not even requested the paperwork.

For the first time, the reality I may never meet her entered my mind. She didn't have to come forward if she didn't want to. The administrator confirmed this fear and told me it was very common for the donor to choose not to contact the recipient.

I was devastated. I needed her to know how grateful we were.

Meanwhile, MAZE continued to draw record crowds, and the show was better than ever. My health was improving, my ability to weave my story through the show was growing, and I was connecting with the audience in a way I'd never before experienced.

I AM SECOND, a Christian organization, heard about my story and shot a short film, capturing what God had done through my life. They posted the video online and immediately people responded to my story.

But I couldn't let it go. I desperately wanted to meet the young lady who'd saved my life. Every couple of weeks, I'd call MD Anderson, hoping my mysterious donor had requested her paperwork.

Nothing.

Every time I performed at a college campus and looked out over the crowd of 18-20 year olds, I thought about my donor. What was her life like? What did she think about me? Did she have any idea how grateful my family was for the gift she'd sacrificed to give us?

Then it dawned on me. I was so overwhelmed by her act of kindness, and there were thousands of people like me, waiting for their match. When audiences heard my story, they were moved. It was time for me to call them to action. If we could build the donor base, we could shrink that one in nine million number and help save lives.

I invited the NMDP to come to our events, and before long, we began to see hundreds of people sign up every night, all across the country. MAZE has become one of the two largest recruiters of new enrollees in the U.S.

What an amazing and humbling privilege—you can see God's fingerprints all over it.

God allowed me to go through my battle with cancer, but He never took His hand off my life. He was there with me for every one of those awful moments at MD Anderson. In His providence, He chose to use my life in some small way to create hope in those waiting for their match and compassion in those who knew nothing about the issue.

Looking back, I can clearly see this was His road for me. As difficult and painful as it was, I've come to the place where I believe my disease was a gift.

Without it, I wouldn't have the relationship I now enjoy with Jesus or the privilege to be a part of the healing process for so many others I'll never meet.

I take no credit for it. I was the mark, and God was the performer.

I wouldn't have it any other way.

♣ ♦ ♥ ♠

Most people don't answer a blocked number during lunch—especially not lunch at Uncle Julio's—but I'm not most people. I couldn't risk passing up the call I'd been waiting months to receive.

It was the NMDP. They simply asked, *"Would you like to know who saved your life?"*

Tears filled my eyes. I struggled to find the composure to answer, *"Yes!"*

They responded, *"We'll send you an email with her information."*

As soon as they hung up, I went to the home page on my phone and stared, waiting for the mail icon to pop up. I stared into the phone like an anxious cook waiting for water to boil, mumbling to myself, *"C'mon ... c'mon!"*

Finally, the envelope icon appeared, and the alert sound went off. I immediately opened the email—all her information was in the form of a scanned PDF. Her handwriting was clearly feminine with bubbly flourishes distinctive enough to be its own font. She lived in Milwaukee, Wisconsin.

Her name was Jennell. I found her on Facebook and sent her a message and a friend request. The message said, *"It's because of you my wife is not a widow. It's because of you my kids are not fatherless. It's because of you I can even type this right now. You saved my life."*

She posted a music video on my page from the band Jack's Mannequin. It was a slow, haunting melody, and I wasn't sure what it meant. She sent me a message, and we arranged a Skype call for later that night.

I was a mess all day. What was I going to say? I asked Eli about the proper etiquette in this situation. Do you buy flowers, a gift card, a new car ... offer a kidney? All of it and more seemed appropriate.

When the three of us finally got on the call together, Jennell told Eli and me about the mysterious song she'd posted.

The lead singer of Jack's Mannequin at that time was a man named Andrew McMahon. He, too, was from Orange County. In 2005, just months before the band's debut album was released, McMahon was diagnosed with Acute Lymphoblastic Leukemia (my initial diagnosis). He'd found a match, and after receiving his marrow transplant, he'd made a full recovery.

Jennell was moved by the amazing act of kindness that saved McMahon's life, and so when she saw a table from the NMDP at the Warped Tour in 2008, she immediately knew she didn't just want to donate ... she wanted to be a match.

She wanted to save someone's life.

In March 2009, she received a call to be my match.

As we communicated through the Skype windows on our computers, I heard pieces of Jennell's worldview seep through. And while it was like many college students I'd met over the years, it wasn't like mine. She was socially conscious, politically liberal, passionately pro-choice, and wonderfully intelligent.

While our bone marrow matched, our worldviews didn't—and yet she did it anyway. Somehow this made her even more special to Eli and me. When she agreed to be the match, she committed to get a tattoo in the shape of a puzzle piece, surrounding the area where the IV went into her arm.

On that unforgettable evening, all the puzzle pieces fell into place.

And this girl, this stranger was my missing piece.

We've had the chance to be together several times since that first night. She's visited us on several occasions, and we always have stimulating conversations. Jennell has been an unforeseen, unexpected blessing to our family.

"Caves," the song she posted on my wall, the song so instrumental in bringing the pieces of our puzzle together, is covered with the mysterious, supernatural fingerprints of God.

It's become one of my favorite songs, too.

♣ ♦ ♥ ♠

*I'm caught*
*Somewhere in between*
*Alive*

*And living a dream.*

*No peace*

*Just clicking machines*

*In the quiet of compazine.*

*The walls caved in on me.*

*And out here*

*I watch the sun circle the earth*

*The marrows collide in rebirth*

*In God's glory praise*

*The spirit calls out from the caves.*

*The walls fell and there I lay*

*Saved.*

# CHAPTER 17

---

# WHAT I FOUND IN THE MAZE

**"For the Son of Man came to seek and to save the lost."**

Jesus, Luke 19:10 NIV

A charlatan is *someone who pretends to have more knowledge or skills in his profession than he actually possesses.* Charlatans prey on the innate human longing to be amazed, to be awed.

We call these people *"marks."* But it's a deal we all make. The charlatan loves the feeling of taking the audience for a ride. And the whole reason the crowd shows up in the first place is because they need to be reminded the world is filled with wonder.

This deal between a storyteller and the audience is often called *"suspension of disbelief."* We know Gotham City is not a real place and there's no billionaire vigilante who dresses up like a flying rodent in order to fight crime, but we're willing to bury those critiques in order to be captivated for a couple of hours.

The power of wonder is why, as a child, I fell in love with magic. It's what I loved about playing the piano. And it was the best part of baseball.

Not everyone likes baseball, but the whole world loves sports because at any time, something incredible and unexplainable can happen.

But you can't be enchanted by wonder without making yourself vulnerable. Sometimes the magician turns out to be a fraud, the storyteller can't deliver on his premise, and the athletic champion is exposed as a cheater.

Wonder takes a beating. Skeptical cynicism barks in our collective ears.

*Grow up! When are you going to face facts? There's no such thing as fairy tales. In the real world, dreams don't come true. Quit being a sucker and confront reality.*

♣ ♦ ♥ ♠

Which brings us back to my story.

When you hear about the last several years of my life, you have different options, but in the end, two separate themselves from the rest.

In option one, I'm a statistical anomaly—the beneficiary of dumb, blind luck fortunate enough to be holding the winning lottery ticket. Sooner or later, the numbers had to come up in someone's favor, and I was in the right place at the right time.

But in option two, my healing has nothing to do with luck or numbers, but instead, every detail of my story was penned and orchestrated by the Master's incomparable hand of providence.

In this account, I'm a living, breathing miracle.

Through my sickness, I received the support of many wonderful, loving friends. Some of these were fellow magicians and illusionists— and every one of them would vote for option one.

My friend Rob stayed with me during some of my most difficult moments at MD Anderson. The quality and character of his friendship was beyond what I deserved or expected, but to this day, he thinks I'm simply fortunate. He understands and respects my perspective, but in his mind, there's no deeper explanation.

Charlatans don't have to try to be skeptics. It's part of the gig. We're trained to spot the misdirection, the sleight of hand, and all the other subtle clues that create wonder in the eye of the uninformed. It's our craft—and ironically, as we get more proficient, the more difficult it becomes for us to ever again experience wonder.

Nearly all the great magicians have lived this way. Houdini's skills were so developed and his showmanship was so compelling, no matter how hard he tried, he couldn't convince one of his friends he had no supernatural powers. This wasn't just any friend—it was Sir Arthur Conan Doyle—the creator of the world's greatest detective, the archetype for every sleuth and mystery solver: Sherlock Holmes.

In our culture, the average person picks option one. It's easier. Skepticism has become our default setting. The cynic automatically takes the intellectual high ground. We don't leave room for the unknown. We're not comfortable with unsolved mysteries.

But skepticism comes with a price. A world without wonder might make sense to our minds, but it leaves us cold and alone. The skeptic trusts only what can be proven scientifically, which sounds great in theory but is miserable in practice.

When was the last time you proved how much you love someone with empirical data?

Option two comes with risks, too. It means we're not in control. No amount of money, power, or influence can protect us from risk.

For all of our education, our technology, and our progress, we're still so small and fragile. If humanism is true, our most talented, most beautiful, most accomplished, and most wealthy would also be our most fulfilled.

But we all know life doesn't work this way.

♣ ♦ ♥ ♠

I understand why the skeptic looks at my life and sees the inexplicable result of chaos. In his mind, there's nothing miraculous about it at all. Over a long enough period of time, sooner or later, somebody's going to pull the winning numbers.

But I'll never be able to see it this way. There are too many glimpses of carefully crafted design. It wasn't enough for God to wink—He knew I needed to clearly see His hand at work in my redemption.

Seriously.

My blood was poisoned and was killing me from the inside out, leaving me with only one hope. My willpower, my determination, my hard work couldn't save my life—only the blood of a perfect match, poured out on behalf of my broken body in order to save me and give me new life.

Out of a nine million person database, there was only one match—who happened to be the very demographic I'd spent my entire professional career serving. And the reason she decided to become a donor was because the lead singer of her favorite band had the same disease.

And by the way, like me, he, too, was from Orange County.

God's fingerprints were everywhere. This message of the saving power of blood comes right out of Scripture.

> "Yet God, with undeserved kindness, declares that we are righteous. He did this through Christ Jesus when he freed us from the penalty for our sins. For God presented Jesus as the sacrifice for sin. People are made right with God when they believe that Jesus sacrificed his life, shedding his blood. This sacrifice shows that God was being fair when he held back and did not punish those who sinned in times past ..." Romans 3:24-25 NLT

This message I'd shared with people for years, this message I'd questioned, doubted, and given up on, turned out to be the foundation for the procedure that literally saved my life.

How else can you respond to that?

Either you shake your fist one final time and walk away forever, or you fall on your knees with a gratitude so strong, you struggle to articulate it.

Like I said before, I chose option two.

Along the way, I started to feel the same way the audience feels at my show. At the beginning of an illusion, they're confused. They don't know what I'm doing. They want to see something amazing, but they don't really trust me.

And then I start working on them, intentionally asking them questions I'm not really concerned about as I move and gesture in dramatic ways I want them to see because they don't know where to look. If they knew where to look, they'd see what I was doing.

But they don't.

Once they start to see where I'm going, it comes across their face, and then they say, *"No way ... no way ..."* All the pieces start to fit together, and things that seemed so random become vitally clear.

I can describe this process so clearly—not because I see people go through it at my shows—it's the way I define these past few years. I found myself saying, *"No way ... no way ... "* over and over.

Today, I can honestly say I've never been more confident in both the goodness and the sovereignty of God. He's got it under control, and His character is better and more beautiful than you can imagine.

Don't hear what I'm not saying. My pain and disappointment, my confusion with the end of my baseball career, my distress over Tennyson's death, and my intense anger with God were real.

I endured many long, dark nights of the soul.

New perspective and a greater understanding of God's larger plan won't turn your deepest wounds into rainbows and butterflies.

Life isn't fair. It often doesn't make sense. It leaves you with scars, bruises, and a limp, if you can walk at all. It's not neat and tidy. It's messy, difficult, challenging, and painful, and yet, there's beauty in every moment.

That's the story of my life. But I'm certainly not alone. The details are never the same, but there's a common theme: *God's more interested in crafting a great story than preventing us from experiencing pain.*

No major character in Scripture was exempt from gut-wrenching pain, from moments of agony, discouragement, confusion, and anger. Faith is tested. Mysteries go unresolved. And then somehow, incredibly, unbelievably, God restores and redeems the situation.

Abram's road from childless patriarch to the father of our faith was filled with heartache, pain, confusion, delayed hope, fulfillment, and even greater challenge.

Jacob was a manipulative joker who was tricked by others until he finally wrestled with God.

In order for Joseph to rescue his people, he was hated and betrayed by his brothers, falsely accused by those he helped, and stuck in a prison hole while guilty men around him were set free.

The list is nearly endless. And don't think for a moment I'm equating myself with the men and women of Scripture. The point is not that I'm great ... God is.

We see this pattern repeated constantly: Possibility. Promise. Suffering. Hope. Injustice. Confusion. Mystery. Redemption. Transformation. Significance. Despite what you may have learned in Sunday school, the purpose of these stories is not to show us how men and women overcame difficult circumstances through great moral character.

These stories show us the goodness and faithfulness of God. He hasn't changed.

I don't need to understand why things happened the way they did in order to see God's sovereignty and goodness covering every area of my life. My cancer—my death became a gift. I never would've picked it, but I wouldn't change it for the world.

♣ ♦ ♥ ♠

When I received my diagnosis, I was shocked, angry, bitter, and unwilling to embrace the reality of it. Now I celebrate my story and share it with thousands of people over and over on a nightly basis.

That's one of the reasons I love what I'm doing. Every night I'm in front of an audience, I get to admit how wrong I was. I get to celebrate God's goodness and His power in spite of my weakness.

And the truth is, my show is so much better with my story than it was without it. The audience connects with my pain and my vulnerability. I'm able to find common ground with a much larger group of people who may not relate to my worldview, but they empathize with my story.

Even the most ardent atheist sees my humanity and not just my ideology when they realize what I've been through. I love finding a point of connection with people who have no desire for empty religion or spiritual games because I feel the same way.

Jesus did, too.

And He also loved the hurting and the broken, the ones everybody else gave up on, the people who felt insignificant, marginalized, and far from Him. He spilled His blood so that they could have a genuine relationship with God ... and so you and I could, too.

If you stop and think about it, expecting college kids to develop a relationship with God because they see a few illusions and hear a story about a guy who survived leukemia is ridiculous.

But it's happening anyway.

I'm so grateful God doesn't wait for us to understand what He's up to in order to move in our lives.

Every night, hundreds of young men and women sign up to become bone marrow donors. Every donor makes the difference between life and death for someone.

Every night people hear the message of the Gospel, see Jesus for Who He truly is, and experience the power of transformation.

And every night, the story of my life gets better.

# EPILOGUE

---

*"The spirituality of wonder knows the world is charged with grace, that while sin and war, disease and death are terribly real, God's loving presence and power in our midst are even more real."*

Brennan Manning

You've heard my story. Now the question is, *"Where is the wonder in your story?"*

I don't know how old you are, where you live, or what you had for breakfast this morning. Well ... actually, I do, but that's not important right now.

You are important.

Your story matters.

Life is a gift. And on many days, it feels like one blends into another with little significance until one day you wake up, wondering where the last few years went.

One of the cruelest ironies about human beings is we all want to be comfortable, and yet, once we're secure, we long for something more.

Something mysterious.

Something awe-inspiring.

If this weren't true, no one would ever come to my shows. Total strangers wouldn't freak out as their minds, their eyes, and their hearts struggle to figure out what they just saw.

Life is too sacred to spend wandering around aimlessly in a maze.

I'm a charlatan. I use magic and sleight of hand to wake people up to the reality that life is bigger than what we can see or perceive through our senses.

Deep down, we already know this.

Please take my word for it. The alternative is much more difficult. In *The Problem of Pain,* C.S. Lewis said, *"God whispers to us in our pleasures, speaks to us in our conscience, but shouts in our pains: It is His megaphone to rouse a deaf world."*

For so many people, the only antidote to the wonderless monotony of daily life is pain. It's amazing how the realities of life-and-death can give us a whole new perspective on life.

Think of me as a pain-free alternative. If you'd like, you can vicariously borrow the gut-wrenching experience of my journey.

- *When was the last time you felt truly alive?*
- *When was the last time life took your breath away?*
- *How long has it been since you got out of bed filled with the unmistakable sense that your life mattered?*

Even as you read these words, you long for them because of the way you were designed. You were created to live with purpose, wide-eyed wonder, and a magical sense of awe.

Think of this as your invitation out of your illusion. Don't settle. There's more waiting for you on the other side.

There's a God Who loves you Who's writing an incredible story through your life. It may be messy, painful, terrifying, and filled with all kinds of uncertainty.

Great stories always are.

It doesn't mean He's given up on you. He's simply setting you up for an incredible reveal. He's inviting you to jump deeper into the mystery. Stop trying to make sense of it, and embrace what He's doing in your life.

Jesus never plays it safe. He never hangs back in the comfortable, mundane place. He hangs out in storms, chases people stuck on the margins, reaches the unreachable, and loves the unlovable.

He meets washed-up baseball players at old converted strip malls, gives them ridiculous dreams, then moves mountains to show His goodness and love in their lives.

If you keep your life safe, you'll never learn the incredible joy and privilege of genuinely trusting Him.

Don't play it safe.

Safe is boring.

Safe can be explained.

Safe never leads to wonder.

Pick up the dream you let go of because you were afraid.

Do something crazy for someone who could never repay you.

Chase a dream so big it invites skeptics to mock you.

When you do, you'll discover the life that's been waiting for you all along.

You don't keep a great story to yourself.
You tell everyone you know.

For tour dates, booking details, and more information,
go to **www.whatisthemaze.com.**

"A BOLD NEW STRATEGY...
THEY CHALLENGE YOUNG PEOPLE TO THINK
ABOUT HOW THEY PERCEIVE THE WORLD,
WHAT'S TRUE...AND WHAT'S NOT..."
-MARK GAUTHIER, NATIONAL DIRECTOR OF CAMPUS MINISTRY,

CAMPUS CRUSADE FOR CHRIST

**IF YOU'RE BETWEEN THE AGES OF 18 AND 44, SOMEWHERE, SOMEONE IS WAITING FOR YOU.**

BE  THE MATCH®

There are thousands of people like Jim, facing a life-threatening illness, waiting desperately for their match.

The National Marrow Donor Program is growing, but the need is great, especially among those of racially or ethnically diverse heritages.

To discover how you can support this incredibly important movement, please visit marrow.org today!

Be the match.
Save a life.